So, You Want to Move to Ghana

What You Need To Know BEFORE You Make the Big Leap

*** Tips, Tools, & Resources included ***

by

Hannah P. Yacob

Copyright © 2021 by Hannah P. Yacob

All rights reserved. No part of this publication may be reproduced, distributed, or transmitted in any form or by any means, including photocopying, recording, or other electronic or mechanical methods, without the prior written permission of the publisher, except in the case of brief quotations embodied in critical reviews and certain other noncommercial uses permitted by copyright law. For permission requests, write to the publisher, addressed "Attention: Permissions Coordinator," at the address below.

Jai Publishing House Incorporated
Promenade II
1230 Peachtree Street NE
19th Floor
Atlanta, Georgia 30309
www.jaipublishing.com

The Publisher is not responsible for websites (or their content) that are not owned by the publisher.

The views expressed in this publication are those of the author and do not necessarily reflect the official policy or position of any other agency, organization, employer or company associated with the publisher.

Printed in the United States of America

ISBN-13: 978-1-7366613-8-3

This book is dedicated to the Creator of all things.

"Trust in יהוה, with all thine heart; lean not unto thine own understanding. In all thy ways acknowledge Him, and He shall direct thy paths. Be not wise in thine own eyes: fear יהוה, and depart from evil. It shall be health to thy navel, and marrow to thy bones."

— Proverbs 3:5-8 Tanakh.

"This page intentionally left blank"

Contents

Introduction 7

Chapter 1
Becoming Legal: Proper Documentation 9

Chapter 2
All About That Paper 20

Chapter 3
How You Living? 35

Chapter 4
Transportation 60

Chapter 5
Nourishment 67

Chapter 6
Shipped Goods & Clearing Customs:
Recommended Do's and Don'ts of
Household Import 71

Chapter 7
Electronic vs. Electric - What? **83**

Chapter 8
Home Country & Ghana Mail **104**

Chapter 9
Obtaining Long-term Residency or Citizenship **107**

Chapter 10
What I Don't Like About Ghana **112**

Chapter 11
Extra Tips **122**

Resources **129**

References **130**

About the Author **132**

Acknowledgments **133**

Introduction

Late 2020, my husband and I embarked on the journey of a lifetime. After one year of planning, we uprooted ourselves from North America and moved to the country of Ghana, located on the West African continent.

Now, truth be told, we had not planned on moving to Ghana until September 2021. However, an unforeseen enemy called Covid-19 reared its ugly head.

Uncertainty concerning future travel rules and restrictions forced us to adjust our planning as not to get trapped on a side of the world we no longer desired to reside.

So, you want to move to Ghana?

Do you really? Have you weighed all of the pros and cons of living on another continent? Before you decide, I will reveal to you unbiased truths about the country: the good, the bad and the ugly.

If you make it half-way through this book, and still seek to relocate to Ghana, the information contained in this book will preserve your sanity by expounding upon quite a few tips that will prove extremely beneficial.

Pour yourself a nice cup of tea, coffee or whatever your pleasure, grab a seat and hold on!

Chapter 1

Becoming Legal: Proper Documentation

First and foremost, if you intend on residing in Ghana, you will have to apply for a National ID and a Work and Residence Permit because the initial visa stay is only valid for a maximum of 90 days.

Some people mistakenly believe that a multiple entry visa with an expiration of 2 to 5 years grants them permission to stay in country for that duration (2 to 5 years pending the visa). However, this is not the case. If you have a 2-, 3- or 5-year visa, this simply means you have the ability to come in and out of Ghana in 90-day increments over a 2- to 5-year period.

If you intend to stay passed the 90-day allotted duration, you must obtain the proper documentation. Now you must be wondering, how does one go about obtaining these documents? No worries, I got ya! Or as we say in Ghana, "I dey fo you."

OBTAIN A NATIONAL IDENTIFICATION (ID) CARD

To obtain your National ID, you simply have to:

1. Go to the National Identification Authority (NIA) building ran by the Government of Ghana;
2. Pay the fee;
3. Get your picture taken/finger printed; and
4. Fill out the required government form.

The form asks general questions such as your address, phone number, previous names (i.e., due to marriage), and occupation. If you resign from your job, move to Ghana and don't know what to put down for occupation, simply put your professional craft or trade.

You can even put entrepreneur if you plan on starting your own business. The ID must be renewed yearly. The initial cost is $120 United States Dollars (USD) per person, regardless of age. The cost to renew is $60 USD.

You can pay in the Ghana equivalent currency of cedis (GHC); however, the currency exchange rate fluctuates daily. As I write this, the initial $120 USD cost would equate to $693 GHC, w/renewal cost at $347 GHC.

To travel to the NIA office, you will need to give your driver (provided you have one) the location of where you are going. Be aware that typical addresses in Ghana are not like those of the West.

For instance, in the West, if you want to go to a certain location, you look up the street address complete with building or house number.

Not so here. If you ask someone for their location, they will give you a region with a roundabout location with land marks to aide you. When you are not familiar with the country, let alone a particular area in that country, this type of address is futile.

No need to fret, Ghana uses a "digital address" also known as "GPS Code" to locate a place or business.

Supposedly every registered home and business in Ghana now has a digital address. All you have to do is ask for the digital address, drop it in Google and voila! You are now no longer lost!

Resource

NIA Digital Address: GA - 237 – 1033
NIA website: https://nia.gov.gh/

Note: *information for obtaining a driver's license Is found here as well*

Once on the NIA website, scroll down and click "Get Your Non-Citizen Ghana card."
Sadly, that link may or may not work. If that link doesn't work, then try this link: https://fims.org.gh/info/where-to-buy-a-card/

Becoming Legal: Proper Documentation | 11

Here you will be able to find locations to obtain the Scratch card (card used to actually pay for the ID), locations for where you can actually register and obtain the actual ID, as well as operating days and hours.

Tip: I personally would only use the NIA or an Immigration Service location.

RECAP

If that is as clear as mud, here is a summary for both initial and renewal of the Non-Citizen ID:

1. Purchase a scratch card (not mandatory but please do so) at an authorized location.
2. Go to a registration location (NIA, Immigration, etc.) to complete the form, pay the fee, pictures and finger prints taken (pointer and thumb), wait about 15-20 minutes for processing and obtain your ID.
3. Must renew yearly. https://fims.org.gh/how-to/renew/

Documents required for initial card: Passport. Note, for initial card the website states that you also need your Residence Permit. This is incorrect.

You actually need a National ID to apply for your Residence Permit. Just ensure you tell them this is your first card, not a renewal and that you need it to apply for your Residence Permit.

You may walk through the initial process via this link: https://fims.org.gh/how-to/register/

Documents required for renewal: Passport, Expiring ID, Residence Permit (which must also be renewed yearly so take care of this a month or so before it expires)

Costs: Initial card is $120 USD. Annual renewal is $60 USD. Don't cry. Yes, I know that hurts. Cost is per person.

Tip: I suggest going to the webpage and taking a screenshot or printing out the locations for registration and scratch card purchase locations prior to coming to Ghana, in case the websites are down during the time you wish to obtain your card.

Recall that I stated above that the Scratch card is not really required but it is best to get one? Well, let me tell you a funny story.

I had no book to read to walk me through all of these processes of what to do and what to expect. I did have amazing Ghanaian brothers to tell me what I needed and for the most part, where to go to obtain what I needed.

However, being citizens, they couldn't tell me exactly what the process entailed. So, I take my happy self to the NIA counter to obtain my Non-Citizen ID.

I was so happy, singing in my head all the way to the counter, "My first step to becoming legal. Lala la la la!" I was handed the proper form to fill out, then paid a fee at the Teller Counter.

I proceeded to have a seat and wait to be called for further processing. Here's where it gets interesting... The Teller, who is taking a nice nap while the young lady next to him is working incessantly, is nudged to provide me service. He asks for my card, but of course, I don't have one because no-one told me I needed one.

He responds, "No problem," and asks me for the proper payment amount. I don't have the exact change so I hand him the money expecting my change. He tells me that he doesn't provide change but that I could request it in the 'processing room'. Yep, just like that, I fell for it.

Please do not let the Teller inform you that you will receive your change once you go through additional processing. He is simply trying to keep your money in hopes that you will forget to retrieve it once you have finished processing and obtained your ID.

If this does happen to you and you ask for your change in the processing room, they will simply have a good laugh at your expense and tell you to retrieve your change from the slick Teller.

Yes, he tried it but I got my money back. This is why I suggest you follow protocol and purchase a prepaid Scratch card to give to the Teller.

I can laugh about it now but when you are new in a country, slightly jet lagged, head in the clouds, don't know what you are doing, feeling like a gerbil on a running mill, it "ain't" so funny!

In reference to having to purchase and carry the ID card, some may say, I don't want a card that has a chip in it with my biometric information (fingerprint, face, signature).

Well, I hate to break it to ya, but if you have a bank card, if you have your country's National ID card, if you have a Passport, if you have a federal ID card, you have a chip!

As long as I'm not being chipped directly on my person, I'm good. I refuse to alter the Father's creation in any abominable way. At least that's my humble opinion. I digress, let's get back to business.

Now that you are equipped with your Non-Citizen National ID, you need to obtain your Work and Residence Permit.

OBTAIN YOUR WORK/RESIDENCE PERMIT

These documents are a lot more complicated to obtain. I know what you are thinking, "Just point me to the right website and I can take it from there." No, not really.

So where do you go, what documents do you need, and how much does it cost to obtain the Work and Residence Permit? First you must obtain a medical checkup (keep your receipt) and gather all required documentation which is as follows:

1. Two (2) passport pictures: best to bring quite a few of these in country
2. Copy of your Non-Citizen ID
3. Curriculum Vitae (CV): Equivalent to the West's resume, although it is more personal. However, care should be taken to conform the CV to a certain profession, trade or business.

   Try and keep its length to 2-3 pages maximum. Administrators don't want to read a book no matter how great and experienced you are. You want to put your best face (on paper face) forward. So update your resume and make it count.

   It is much easier to do if you tailor it to your profession. If you are like me and have held quite a few professional positions over the course of many years, you will have to hone it in on what skill sets matter most to you, and from what skill sets you believe Ghana may benefit.

   Don't stress over it but don't take it lightly either. Remember that issuance of a Work and Residence Permit to remain in country is a privilege if granted, not a right.
4. Police Report from home country. This report can be obtained online for $20 to $25, pending your state. Just do a search for your state-specific police report. Ensure you print it or save to PDF. If you don't, you may have to pay again to obtain your document.

   I do believe the report can't be more than 30-ish days old, but don't quote me on that. Again, do your due diligence to research based on your specific needs.
5. Any relevant professional certificates (e.g., Teacher Certification) and degrees. If you can't locate the actual

degree/certificate, submit the transcript showing the degree earned. DO NOT forget to redact anything showing your Social Security Number (SSN)! Always use a TIN (Tax ID Number) or National/Non-Citizen ID Card number. Never, ever give up your SSN on any documentation!

6. If you have already obtained work from an employer, submit a copy of your employer's work contract.

7. If you will be your own employer (have a registered business), submit a copy of your company's incorporation certificate and all regulations.

8. If you will be working for your own company, you must submit an Application for work/residence permit letter on company letterhead (see Resources). You type this yourself, for yourself (or others if they will be working for you) on behalf of your company.

9. Medical Report from a GIS clinic

10. Completed Work Permit form (obtain at office free; needed even if you are opening a business)

11. Completed Residence Permit Form (obtain at office free)

12. Your original passport. Yes, that's right, you gotta give it up. You will be given a receipt to carry while your documents are being processed. Just as your Visa becomes a part of your passport, so will your Work and Residence Permit.

Keep a copy of your receipt as well as your Non-Citizen ID with you at all times. You will usually receive your passport back complete with your Visa, which is now also your Work and Residence Permit in about 24-28 days.

I have known folks to obtain it in 2 weeks but that is rare

WHERE TO OBTAIN THE REQUIRED FORMS AND SUBMIT YOUR PACKAGE?

First things first, you need to ensure you have enough money. As of the release of this book, you need CASH, no debit or credit. Ghana is mostly a Cash society. Cash is king here!

Your upfront medical costs will be around $1,100 GHC. Your application fee is $1000 USD. If you are not paying in U.S. Dollars, as I write, that fee would be $5,780 GHC. For a total of $6,880 GHC per person.

Okay, once you have all your documentation and needed IDs together, take everything to the Ghana Immigration Service (GIS) in Accra for submittal, payment, and processing. Once you obtain your Residence Permit, you may apply for Dependent Residence for any of your dependents, e.g., a spouse, children under age 18, and parents over age 60.

For dependents, submit two passport size photos, passport, copy of Non-Citizen ID, Birth Certificate (for children), Marriage Certificate (for spouse), Application letter on Company's letterhead (if working for someone or own a business) requesting the dependent Residence Permit.

If you are retired and don't plan on working or have a registered NGO (I pray it's nonprofit), you do not have to obtain a Work Permit to remain in Ghana; you will just need to get your Residence Permit. In this case, you will still need all the above documents minus the CV (Resume) and business information.

OBTAIN YOUR TIN

Supposedly Ghana is going away from the required TIN and moving towards using the National ID[3] (Non-Citizen ID for foreigners). Yet, they still need it for conducting quite a bit of business (e.g., opening a bank account, registering land, etc.).

So just apply for your TIN. I obtained mine before moving to Ghana. It's quick and easy. You may apply via the Ghana Revenue Authority at https://gra.gov.gh/tin/.

Some organizations will provide all these services on your behalf and charge you thousands of dollars. Wouldn't that money be better spent on the actual fees needed to acquire the documents without additional costs? Besides, you could use all that extra money to start a business in-country. Oh yes, we will get to that shortly.

Ah, look at you! You might feel like a walking ATM, but on the bright side, congrats, you're officially a legal resident!

You are now equipped with your National ID, TIN, and Work and Residence Permit. You're really getting things done. So now what?

Well, if I were you and I didn't have a retirement check at my disposal, I'd be earnestly trying to get some cash flow rolling in. We don't want to deplete those savings accounts any more than we have to.

Flip on over to Chapter 2, so we can continue our discussion.

Chapter 2
All About That Paper

If you are not a retiree with a monthly check, or a trust fund baby, you need income and fast! If you have income rolling in and are in chill mode, proceed to Chapter 3. For all remaining readers, this chapter is for you.

One must decide whether to work for someone else or go into business for one's self. Unless you have a highly sought after skill or profession that is in short supply in Ghana (e.g., doctor, nurse, Scientist, teacher, etc.), you need to establish your own business.

Seriously, there are plenty of unemployed college graduates here who had to return home and live with mom and dad, just like in the West.

So what can you do? Do your homework and determine what's needed in the regional area that you can afford to lease purchase land in or rent (also known as 'Let') a business space.

Soul search and determine what you are good at, what you are passionate about and do it! That's one of the great things about Ghana... it's a developing country so business opportunities are endless!

You just need to plan wisely and get in where your skill set fits in. You don't have to be a millionaire to start a business in Ghana, you just have to be smart and resourceful.

Even if you just start your business and hire just 2-3 reliable Ghanaians, that is 2-3 people that are now gainfully employed thanks to your business development.

Ensure you have an employee handbook (set the work standard) and stand by it. Be firm, but fair.

If starting your own tangible business gives you the "heebie geebies," consider an online business idea. You could also be a "hands off" investor. Meaning, you invest in someone else's business for a return on investment.

Tip: *Have a lawyer look over the proposal for you to ensure everything is on the up and up.*

Let's walk through the process for registering a business in Ghana.

1. Decide the type of business you want to set up. I don't just mean whether you want to open a restaurant or produce bath and body products. What I'm referring to here is the type of business structure you wish to have (i.e. sole proprietorship, limited liability company, partnership). You will need this information to complete the forms.
2. Choose a business name. Must do a name check to ascertain the name you have selected is not already in use by a registered business.
3. You will need a business address. Use the address where you are currently living and update later, or get a local Post Office Box. If you go the P.O. Box route, make certain you place your eyes on the P.O. Box key. Don't go through the process, pay the fee, just to be told that they can't locate the key or that they will give the key to you upon your initial visit to check your box. What will likely happen is since you never received a key, your mail will be held for ransom each time you go to collect it until you give a small "donation" to the clerk. This little dance could drag on for months. If the clerk states they can't locate a key for your box, insist on another box that has a key or opt not to rent a box. *Hey, I promised to tell you the good, the bad and the ugly.*
4. You will need a business email address. Your mailing address and email address will be utilized as means of contact for your business.
5. Identify your director and secretary positions. There will be forms both the director and secretary have

to complete and sign. If you are a small business, these positions will typically be the owner(s). Two directors are required for a business. However, one of the directors may also serve in the role as secretary.

6. Determine your startup capital. Keep in mind that as a foreigner, you are required to eventually show $500,000 USD country investment over time. Don't have a heart attack just yet.

How this works: if you put down $50,000 USD startup capital on your forms, this means over "x" amount of years, you must eventually show the investment of $450,000 USD in country business investment. Whatever amount you put on the forms, keep in mind that you must be audited once a year. You must contact an auditor (listing provided by the Register's Office once your business registration has been approved) and have this done. Yes, yet another expense.

But this audit is not costly at all. Once you have the audit done (this is after you register the business), you will submit the given form with your bank statements (redacted of sensitive information) and a completed Ghana Investment Promotion Centre (GIPC) form to the GIPC. Once approved, they will provide you with a GIPC Certificate. Now you are all set. You can then use this certificate to obtain a bank account for your company's funds.

Resource:

Ghana Investment Promotion Centre (GIPC) links: htttps://www.gipcghana.com/ and https://gipc.gov.gh/

Some banks do not require the GIPC Certificate, just your business signed/sealed Certificate of Incorporation and the business articles of regulation/association. I actually **highly encourage you** to visit the GIPC office prior to even registering a business as they have many tools and resources available to assist you with business concerns. There is even an entire office dedicated to assist those of the Diaspora who wish to invest in Ghana.

7. Take all documentation and pay to register your business via the Register Generals Office.

Resource:

https://www.rgd.gov.gh/index.html

Don't be overwhelmed by this process. The folks at the Register Generals Office are very friendly and helpful despite the fact that they have mounds of documentation to review and process. I was truly blown away by their patience and courtesy despite their workload.

Don't be intimidated. Usually you will be approached by a security guard who will direct you where you need to go. One last thing, be patient. They are very busy. If you feel you have been waiting way too long, poke your head back into the person's office you have been directed to (as you will be seated in the hall), and remind them that you are still there. It's a busy place, but it's all good.

How much does it cost to register a business in Ghana? Glad you asked! At the time of this publication, in 2021, the cost is $2500 USD cash - not debit or credit - to be paid in US dollars not GHC. That being said, when figuring out how much cash you need to bring, plan accordingly.

By the way, one person can bring in country $10,000 USD but no more than this amount. Please don't be afraid to bring your cash. No one is going to take your money at the airport. Ghanaians want you to come open businesses to create jobs and help Ghana grow.

Bank accounts and how they work

Sigh...some things the West have beautifully simplified to perfection; the banking processes is one of them. Not so much in Ghana. The banking process is convoluted but I'm told it is done as to protect your assets.

Summary of banking: You obtain a bank account by first getting your TIN, Work and/or Residence Permit and Non-Citizen ID. Some banks also require two passport size photos and proof of residence (utility bill or lease agreement attained from land lord). After which you go to the bank of your choice or call to have a representative come to your home or meeting place (e.g., a local mall or restaurant).

I told you, Ghanaians are very personable. If you chose to meet outside the bank, the representative will bring the forms you will need to read over, complete and sign. That is, if you decide to open an account with this particular bank.

The representative should not be asking you for any money as you do not yet have an account.

> ***Never*** *give money to any bank representative outside the bank. This isn't a problem here, just making that clear.*

The representative will process your documents with the bank and will contact you if any additional forms are needed and to inform you of whether or not your account has been approved. Make sure you are also given a "Waiver of Confidentiality/Data Protection For U.S. Person" to read and sign as well. The bank will not be able to grant you use of an account without having this form for you on file. It gives them the right to report monies received from the U.S. by you (if you are a U.S. citizen) into their bank for mandatory IRS reporting. The form clearly states that it is for compliance with the Foreign Account Tax Compliance Act (FATCA).

Now you may go to the bank and deposit your money into your account(s) or transfer money to your account(s) if you have elected e-banking. The representative you initially met with inside or outside the bank will be your primary banking point of contact. You contact this person for all of your banking needs. Due to this, make sure the bank branch you visit or the representative sent to you by the bank works at the branch closest to you.

You are always free to go to another branch but the other branch will always default back to your assigned bank branch representative, giving him or her a call before doing anything on your behalf, which takes up more of your valuable time. Make sure you also request and receive a checkbook (for a small fee) for any account you will be manually withdrawing money from, which is usually done for large quantities that exceed what you can get from an ATM.

Bank account types

1. Current (also known as checking account)
2. Savings

There are various kinds of current accounts pending bank of choice. Of course the typical Current Account is the basic one in which you will maintain GHC. However two other Current accounts to be aware of are the FCA and FEA Current accounts.

Foreign Currency Account (FCA): This is offshore currency (USD, British Pound, Euro), transferred into Ghana that one wishes to remain as foreign currency. This is beneficial if you have a company in Ghana and you transfer foreign funds into it so the funds do not depreciate in value and you will be doing business transaction wires. However, it must be noted that banks do charge a fee if you ever come to the bank to withdraw this type of funds.

Foreign Exchange Account (FEA), also known as Forex Account: Used by companies and individuals who generate foreign currency in Ghana.

In addition to the individual Current account one may acquire, other Current account types that may be opened include corporate, student, and special group accounts (e.g., NGOs, foundations, churches, etc.).

Typical Ghana banking fees:

- $10 GHC monthly maintenance fee
- $3 GHC monthly fee for each debit/credit card issued per person

Note: *if you elect to obtain both a Visa and MasterCard for an account, you will incur a separate monthly fee for both cards.*

So how do you withdraw your money aside from the ATM for larger sums? This is where the headache comes in. In the West you deposit your money, withdraw your money. Transfer money from one of your bank accounts to another one of your bank accounts. You get a text or email from your withdrawal bank that your transfer has been processed, and you may get a text or email when your money hits your receiving bank account. It's that simple.

Not so, initially in Ghana.

So when you do your first international wire transfer of funds (for a fee) from the U.S. to your Ghana account, you will have upfront red tape. Your home country bank will tell you when your money should arrive. You then contact your Ghana bank representative and inform him/her how much you have coming and when it should arrive. The Ghana bank representative should contact you to inform you on when the money hits the Bank of Ghana, <u>not your bank</u>. Now you have to request your money from the Bank of Ghana to be placed in your account.

To do this you write a simple letter constructed as follows:

DATE HERE

The Manager
"INSERT YOUR BANK NAME HERE"

Dear Sir,
Purpose of Transfer

I "INSERT YOUR FULL NAME" of account number "INSERT ACCOUNT NUMBER" am expecting an inflow of $_____USD into this account from myself via "INSERT NAME OF BANK MONEY HAS BEEN TRANSFERRED FROM."

Please credit my account as such.

"SIGN YOUR NAME HERE"
Billy Bob III

You can type this out if you have the means at this point, or you can write and sign it on plain notebook paper. Give it to your representative to send to the Bank of Ghana on your behalf. You will also fill out and sign both a Beneficiary Ownership Form (BOF) and a Purpose of Transfer (POT) document. After doing all of this, do you get to walk out of the bank with your money if you want some or all of it? Nope, the process can take up to 4 hours!

Here is what I suggest. Unless you are going to be out and about in your bank's general area, don't bother going to the bank to request your funds. Your representative can call you when Bank of Ghana transfers your funds and the money is credited to your account. You can also check your account online (if you elect e-banking).

Now, let's go get your money.

Scenario #1: Okay, you arrive at the bank early I hope, so you don't have to wait in line or have to sit in your designated Covid-19 approved outside canopy covered seating. Once you are inside, do not go to the counter. You need to see your representative seated at his/her desk. If your representative is not there you may see another non counter desk seated representative.

You fill out and sign the BOF and POT. Now you have to use your checkbook and write a check to yourself for the requested amount you are withdrawing. The representative takes your check and this time hopefully you get your money.

One of the reasons you may not get your money is because the amount you want to withdraw is not allowed. You may get only the limit withdrawal and will be told to come back for the balance later that day. This is still too much drama.

Let's do a rewind on the play so you can get all your money and tend to your business.

Scenario #2: You email or text (via encrypted means) your bank representative the required letter requesting your funds from the Bank of Ghana. Your representative informs you that the money is in your account or you can check it online yourself. You then call your representative a day before or hours before you want to withdraw any of your funds and tell him or her the large quantity you are requesting, as well as the time you wish to pick up your funds.

When you get to the bank, you skip the line and tell the guard at the door that you have an appointment with your representative. If your representative is free or there is space available inside, the guard will let you inside the bank. You complete and sign the BOF and POT. You complete, sign and give your check to your representative that validates it. Now you can go to the counter and get ALL the money you wanted from your account. No headache, no long waiting.

Tip: Bring a bag or large closable envelope just in case the bank is out of large envelopes.

Although this process is tedious compared to the West, it is a safe process. Let's say you did request funds initially from your home country and the money bypassed the Bank of Ghana and went straight to your account. Only you are told it never reached your account. Where are my funds? I am now screwed internationally.

Because Ghana seeks to protect your money and their reputation, the Bank of Ghana is the central point for all country transfers. This is why they have you personally request your money initially from them for the specific amount you have transferred, so there are no issues.

In my experience via my bank, this is just a one-time headache process as long as you are transferring funds from the same home country bank to the same Ghanaian bank. As you transfer money to the same bank and account in the future, you will be able to just contact your bank representative (do it the day before or hours before if possible) and inform him/her of the amount you will be withdrawing and when you wish to pick it up. They will have your request waiting for you with very little waiting time, if any pending the time of day you visit the bank.

Some banks make you write a check to yourself each time you wish to withdraw your funds, others do not. In this case, you will want to purchase a checkbook even though you don't intend on writing checks for any purchases. Instead, you will utilize the checkbook for withdrawing your funds.

If you don't purchase the checkbook, the bank will provide a check for you each time you come to the bank to withdraw funds, at a higher fee of course.

While we are on banking, you need to sit down with your home country bank and have a heart to heart about what offshore services they have. You may find that you need to shop for an alternate bank or open another account just for handling your Ghana banking needs.

What *do I mean by this?*

Let's say that you need to transfer $50,000 to a personal or business account you have opened in Ghana. Well, some banks will not do international wires and some will not do them to certain countries.

Others that will do an international wire transfer may have a small transfer limit. You may need one account that you like that you keep your money in because you earn great interest on your money each month but they don't do international wires. You wouldn't want to lose out on all that good interest. So you will have to open another home country account that does large international wires. Just make certain you will be able to add this new bank to your good interest earning bank so you can then transfer funds to your new bank that will allow you to do international wires to your Ghana account.

Wow, *that was a mouthful!*

Yet, all these things must be analyzed and planned carefully before making life changing moves. If that was as clear as mud, let me explain it this way.

I have a home country bank I love. It doesn't do international wires or only does small transfers. I don't take out all of my money and move it to a new home country bank.

Instead, I open an account with a great bank that does large international wires and doesn't give me lots of hassles. I can in-turn transfer money from the bank I love as I need to, in order to have the money transferred to my Ghana account for my business needs or personal needs.

Note *that some banks in home country will not let you transfer your own money from one bank to another bank.*

Good questions to ask your existing bank(s):

- Do you do non-business international wires?
- If yes, do you have a limit?
- What is the process for having money transferred internationally either to my account or to someone else?
- Can I do online transfers of my money from my other bank as needed to my account at this bank in the event that I open an account with you?
- Will I be able to transfer money from my account at your bank to another home country account I have?
- What are your international wire fees? (I have heard of them being anywhere from $14 to $30)
- Do you have the scan by phone, deposit check option? This is a HUGE plus! If someone or a company sends you a check to your digital mailbox, you will be able to download a picture of that check, take a picture of it via your phone using your banks remote check deposit option, and it will be deposited into your account. So convenient!

Still with me? Can't shake you? Wow, you must be Ghana bound!

Meet you in chapter 3 where I am going to talk about "how you living."

Chapter 3

How You Living?

Now that you know what is needed for you to reside legally and thrive financially in Ghana, it's time to focus on where you wish to abode.

This decision needs to be well thought out, taking into consideration various elements that are essential to you. First and foremost, one must take note of the available budget with which to work.

DO NOT come to Ghana thinking that for a low cost you are going to build a big home with all the Western amenities, bells and whistles!

Yes, you can build it, but it will cost you. In some instances you will have to import some of the things you may want for the home, and those costs add up as well. If you want it, you can have it, but first ask yourself, how much am I willing to pay?

Other things to consider:
1. Do you want to live near where you intend to start a business?
2. What region of Ghana appeals to you? This means you need to do your homework on the regions of Ghana, their individual location, climate, cost of living, etc.
3. Prefer inner city life, suburbs, countryside or "in the cut" (also known as the village)?
4. Prefer a home or apartment?
5. Rent versus purchase?
6. Consider waste management. Like most of Africa, Ghana has a waste management problem. Why? A whole lot of people, a whole lot of plastic and not enough waste and recycle facilities throughout all the regions.

In addition, the poor who have land, but do not have the money to pay for trash pickup, litter the streets and or burn their trash. Burning would appear to be a good alternative, but when you burn plastic outside of properly equipped facilities, it gives off unhealthy toxic fumes.

If you live in a rural setting that isn't occupied by a majority of upscale homes and businesses, you will have the poor living in your area. This means that you will have to deal with the fumes, and plastic doesn't burn smelling of roses.

Keep in mind, just like anywhere else in the world, living in the city will provide you with all the comforts you are used to and you have direct access to many businesses, but it costs a whole lot more.

Remember, you are not on vacation; this is where you plan to live. So plan accordingly.

Also find out if there are any issues in a region you seek to live (e.g., high crime, major flooding, lack of medical amenities you may need, etc.). You know what you ultimately can and cannot do without. So consider all these things before making critical decisions.

Be realistic with yourself; for most this will be a lifestyle change. If you have plenty of money to burn, then you can have $450 dollar tailor suits made, smoke high priced cigars, hang out at expensive restaurants and stores, blah, blah, blah…

Yet, for the average person, you are moving to Ghana to get away from all that "keep up with the Jones" nonsense. Ghana is a place where one can work for one's self, create jobs for others, raise a family in a mostly wholesome environment (no place is perfect), and enjoy friends and family.

Things do not move at the rapid pace of the West here in Ghana. Yet, you do not just earn a "living" in Ghana, you actually live. And yes, if you do well financially and have extra "coint" to play with, then by all means, treat yourself!

Ghana has plenty of luxuries at your disposal (e.g., resorts, spas, luxury Airbnbs, restaurants, private amenities, etc.). In a nutshell, do not come to Ghana with unrealistic expectations concerning the cost of living when you are not willing to make sacrifices on some things, overspend, go broke, just to have to move back to the West.

Nobody wants to go down that road, so please, please think before you act, plan and budget wisely!

A few last tips when considering where to live: Communication and labor. If you have or may be considering an online business, go to school online or just need to keep in touch with loved ones, you will need to live somewhere you can get good internet access and tower transmission (phone reception). The closer you live to the towers, the better the reception. If you plan to live in a highly rural, in the cut or mountain area, you will need to research a local phone and internet plan that will enable you to get good reception.

Tip: *AirtelTigo and Vodaphone are both pretty good for rural and some mountainous locations.*

Since we are on the topic of communication, don't forget to invest in a good home country international phone plan. Check with your current carrier and ask for all its options. There may be some plans the company may not be aware of such as professional business or active duty/veteran international plans, etc.

If possible, you want to be able to make free Wi-Fi calls to your home country or incur very little additional costs when you make calls back to your home country to speak with loved ones, take care of business, etc.

WhatsApp is good for calling friends and family as long as they also have the app, but the reception isn't always that good, and calls can sometimes be spotty or drop altogether.

In addition, if you don't already have one, you need to purchase a virtual private network (VPN) before leaving your home country. If you don't use a VPN, you may not be able to access certain websites, as they are country sensitive. Plus it's much safer surfing the net via VPN.

Sometimes even U.S. websites can be quirky. If you are in Ghana using VPN and a U.S. site will not let you in, you may have to sign off of your VPN, and log on to your account (if applicable). Once logged on then you can reconnect to your VPN.

Resource: ProtonMail (protonmail.com) has great VPN options — if you don't already have the option to purchase VPN through any service you are already utilizing.

When it comes to labor, I am referring to the cost to build a home. For instance, if you decide on a mountainous or hilly location, the cost for labor may be higher as the contractors will have to dig through (sometimes blast through) a lot of rock before they can lay the foundation and construct the fencing around the home.

Be mindful that the beauty of living in the mountains may come at a cost. It is doable on a sound budget. You will just have to make tradeoffs such as a smaller floorplan, and the purchase of just one lot (plot of land typically 70x100 ft) instead of many lots.

Do not make tradeoffs when it comes to certain things like the in-home lighting you plan to have, or plumbing, thinking that you can just come back later and add some more ceiling fans, additional recessed lighting, additional Air Conditioners (AC), etc., when you get more money.

Don't buy the additional ceiling fans, light fixtures, AC, but do have the plumbing and electrical wiring ran (via conduit) where you need it to be for future hookup. If you don't, the workers will have to chisel through your wall to run wire and/or pipe for plumbing. This is costly and unsightly as almost all homes are made of cement block. After all that chiseling you will have to pay to have your walls filled in and replastered, and painted again.

When you are having your house built, have all your pipe ran and your wire put in conduit (PV pipe). That way in the future, you'll be able to access your pipe and or wires to hook up everything you need to.

Now, I can see your brain churning and thinking, *Well, I'll just have me a traditional home built and get me some sheetrock walls.* Oh really!? The abundant termites here will have their suitcases packed and be moved into their new resort (your home), so fast it'll make your head spin!

Purchasing Land

If you decide you don't want to rent an apartment or rent/buy a home already built, then you have the option to build. First, you will need to acquire land in which to build your home.

Land is serious business in Ghana. You have to know what you are doing or go through someone you trust who does or you may get seriously burnt!

Getting scammed isn't just something that happens to foreigners, it happens to Ghanaian citizens as well because, as of 2021, the Lands Commission does not yet have a fully automated database.

Don't be discouraged or fearful. You just have to be knowledgeable on the land terminology and the process.

There are technically 4 types of land as recognized by the Ghana Lands Commission: 1. Stool land 2. Family land 3. State land and 4. Public land.

Locals will tell you that there are two types of land: Public Land and Customary land. Customary land is land that belongs to stools, families, skins, clans, or folks that belong to a common ancestral lineage.

Most land in Ghana is Customary land. I am going to give you a breakdown of the Customary land. However, keep in mind that when you go to register Customary land that you purchase, it will be considered either Stool or Family land,

and it is important to know which one you purchase because the registration process is different.

Customary Land

Common Law Freehold: Land that both members of the community and strangers (non-land owning community member Ghanaian) can acquire.

Customary Freehold: Land that individuals or groups hold and is owned by the larger traditional community itself. In this case, the holders of the land are members. This land is transferable to successors or subjects (dependent, subservient) of the individual or subgroups until such time that there are no successors.

Other common terms used:

Stool land: Customary land held by a Stool Chief. The Stool Chief is one who runs the tribal community, represents the community, and looks after the interests of the community. There are smaller chiefs but there is always a head Stool Chief. It is important to understand which chief you are dealing with.

Family land (also known as Private land): Customary land held by an actual family.

Government land (also known as State land): Land the government has acquired in the country.

Public land: Land vested in the President on behalf of and in trust of the Ghanaian people as based on the provisions of the Administration of Lands Act, 1962 (Act 123). Public land also includes other land acquired through the State Lands Act of 1962 (Act 125) or through any other statues in interest of the public.

Leasehold: Acquisition of land by lease for a specific time frame with a start and end period which can be subject to payment of annual rent pending the language of the indenture. If the land you have acquired does not have a building or home on it, make them change the language of the indenture as you should not have to pay an annual or monthly fee of raw land you have lease purchased for "x" amount of years.

There are other minor contractual land types for things such as share cropping but I do not know enough about these types of contracts to be of any benefit. Just know that they do exist in case you seek to lease land in the future for sharecropping or outright farming.

Vested land: Plots of land that is owned by the state and customary authorities in a partnership.

Allodial/Allodia Title: Land title held by only traditional leaders, families or the government. This is the highest land title recognized by Ghanaian law.

Before purchasing any land, the Ghana Lands Commission highly suggests that you first come to them and conduct a search. Conducting a search means that you are researching whether or not there is any recorded transaction or record for which someone other than the person selling you the land holds title and interest to said land.

For Stool and Family land, it is recommended to do a search at the Public Vested Land Management (PVLM) Division. For Family land, an additional search is also recommended via the Survey Mapping Division of the PVLM.

How to register Stool, Family, or State land

All land: If you purchase land that is one acre or more (called bigger land), the land must be assessed and its current value ascertained prior to you being able to register your land.

Stool land: You've purchased or have been given your land directly from a Stool Chief. You must first "conquer" the property before you can continue with the land registration process. Conquer here means that you must go to the PVLM Division located at the Ghana Land Commission and obtain its (Lands Commission) endorsement and record your document in its records. Then you may proceed with the registration process through the Land Commission.

Family land: You've purchased your land from a family. All you have to do is take your indenture to the Lands Commission and go through the Land Title Registration process to obtain your certificate of title.

State land: You've acquired state land. Like Stool land, State land is also managed by the PVLM Division of the Lands Commission. The PVLM will perform the land allocation process of the land to you. Unlike Stool land (one obtains land from the Chief), State land is only purchased through the PVLM Division. This means you CANNOT purchase State land from a family, any security or any other means except through the PVLM Division.

Please note that you will not obtain a conquer or a Title and Registration the same day that you submit your requests and documentation. There is a waiting period. Standard time for Title and Registration is 6 months.

Why does it take so long? Good question. It takes 6 months because the Lands Commission must post the property in the newspaper to ensure no one else has any form of ownership (i.e., another family member).

Do you have to register acquired land? Yes. It is in your best interest to register your land. If you don't you risk it being sold right out from under you. How is this possible, you are wondering? If you fail to register your land, it could be illegally sold again to another person. Now you and the other person have a receipt and a land indenture from the owner. However, when the land goes through the litigation process, the holder of the indenture who first registered the land will be the rightful owner. For all this and additional information your point of reference should always be the Land Commission itself.[5]

As a non-citizen purchasing land in Ghana, I want to make one thing very, very clear... you cannot outright own any land.

As of now, only Ghanaian citizens can own land outright (also known as free hold). As a non-citizen, the "purchase" of land means that you have legally acquired the right to "lease hold" the land for 50 to 99 years.

If you obtain citizenship in the future, you can go to the Lands Commission and have the land registered with all rights of a citizen if your indenture was written as such.

If you are very young, could this come back to bite you in the booty? Absolutely! If you are say, 30 years old and you do a lease hold of 50 years with the option to renew at the 49-50 year mark for another 50 years because you want to pass down the property to your children, you may be in tears to discover that legally, as of 2021, you may have to purchase your property again or at least pay a percentage rated via the economy at that time.

If you have built a home on it, the land lord (person you did the lease hold with or his/her heir) may also charge you rent for the home you built on the property. Is this fair, especially for those who are returning of the Diaspora due to the Transatlantic or other Slave Trade initiated from Africa? No, it is downright ludicrous!

Where this is concerned, Ghana has got to do much, much better or the country risks those who would come and/or invest in Ghana looking elsewhere.

If Ghana is advertising a decade of return, it needs to be a fair return in which returnees' invested homestead sweat, efforts, and investment in the country can be legally passed on to their children, who will in-turn continue to happily invest in Ghana's future. If not, the children of the returned may very well leave the country for greener, fairer pastures and never look back.

In addition, the cost of documentation (Work/Residence Permit) to legally stay in Ghana until citizenship or long term permanent residency is obtained should be greatly reduced for those returning of the Diaspora due to the horrific enslavement of their ancestors and continued discrimination where their ancestors were sold world-wide.

Come on Ghana, let's fix these ugly issues so all may benefit long term!!

If you do purchase land, fence in your property and build on it! The not-so-honest have been posing as realtors or land owners and ripping the unsuspecting buyer off. Is this legal? Of course not, but who wants to go through the hassle of a visit to the register's office where you have to listen to some poor soul cry over money he or she lost due to an illegal sale, or deal with encroachers because you didn't do your due diligence to mark (make sure it's in concrete during survey) and fence your property?

To add to this, if someone moves on your property they will have squatter's rights. You will then have to go through the legal system to have them served with notice stating they must be gone within 30 days.

You want to ensure you purchase from someone credible and the land has been thoroughly vetted. Buy from someone you know and trust! If you insist on going it alone, work directly with the "Stool" Chief of the land (if purchasing Stool land) to obtain your indenture (deed/contract).

I would also suggest having the unsigned indenture looked at by a lawyer prior to any exchange of funds.

If you decide to sell your property, pending on how your indenture is written, you may have to go back to the Stool Chief and give him first dibs at redeeming the land prior to your deed being up. This is your Deed of assignment (time you have left remaining on the property).

The Lands Commission will take your original indenture and place the new indenture along with it. Keep in mind that all chiefs are not just. Okay, maybe that wording is not too fair. What I should say is that you must be mindful of local customs. The chief may want a percentage of what you sell the property for.

Yes, really! If a chief wants 5-10% of the price of sale that's not so bad as it is customary to give something. But anything in excess of that is extortion. Remember, you are not a citizen, so your indenture is actually a ground's lease for "x" amount of years. Be extremely cautious and know from whom you purchase your "lease hold" land.

Please note that you can have your indenture agreement written (it will be unsigned by the owner at this point) prior to you purchasing the land.

IT IS YOUR RIGHT!

If you don't like the terms of the potential lease don't purchase the land. If you purchase land and do not plan to build anytime soon, make sure your indenture contract doesn't have a stipulation as to how soon you have to build. If it does, ensure you start building during the terms of the lease or the actual owner does legally have the right to resell the land you believe to be yours.

Starting to feel like a walking ATM dispensing money? I feel ya pain, but hey, you can't expect to go live in another country and not abide by their customs, rules and processes. After all, you are not seeking to be tourist, but an actual resident.

Also, keep in mind that although the U.S. is a so called "free hold" land country, do you really own land you purchase? No. Why do I say this? You purchase land in the U.S. and you believe it's yours. Well, you fail for whatever reason to pay your taxes or miss your mortgage payments. Now your so called "free hold" land that you thought you owned outright is suddenly gone bye-bye! Your land now belongs to the state or a U.S. bank.

In Ghana, you won't get pushed off your lease hold land, nor will the Ghanaian citizens get pushed off of their free hold land right away. The country works with you. In addition, once your lease hold is up, the land goes back to the family that owns it (just like in the Bible during the Jubilee Year, Lev 25 Tanakh) and not in the hands of other countries or even the Ghanaian government. There are pros and cons no matter where one chooses to live.

Building a home

When it comes to building a home in Ghana, it is work! It is not like building a home in the U.S. or U.K. In the West, if you don't have your own land, you simply pick a lot in the builder's community you wish to live, pick your home plan that already has the costs laid out. From there all you have to do is pick out your colors and any upgrades you want. Once it's built, final paperwork is signed. You get your key and move right in.

In Ghana, once you have your land, you meet with an architect of your choosing to select the house plan. Then you must meet with a structural engineer to ensure your plan is sound (if your home will be 2 or more stories). You will also need a good, trustworthy construction manager to oversee your home building project.

What you spend will depend on the square footage of your home and all the bells and whistles you want included. You also need to pay for a survey and soil topography. The surveyor will also ensure exact points are laid out so your excavation goes smoothly. Understanding what type of soil you are working with is essential to the building process.

For instance, if you want to have your foundation dug to 6 feet, but at 5 feet on your land the soil is too soft and unsupportive of the type of home you are building, the excavator with either have to dig past the soft soil (which costs more), or dig to only 4 feet instead. This is just a simple example but not knowing topography could be disastrous and end up costing you tremendously.

At this point you will be given a breakdown of the materials and labor costs.

Then you are at the point when you pay to have your land cleared and then excavated. Once excavation is complete, the building of your home begins in phases. You will be given a breakdown of all the phases and the cost of each phase upfront in a Priced Bill of Quantities.

There are two ways you can obtain a Priced Bill of Quantities: by contract or by labor. By contract is the breakdown by the month for "x" amount of months they expect to accomplish building your home. It is broken down by each building phase.

However, things like the cost of labor is done by the month, not by the job. The materials costs are also not spelled out in explicit detail, and costs are usually given in USD. With the labor contract, you get a detailed breakdown of all materials and labor costs for each building phase. Costs for this type of contract is given in GHC. If there is something you do not understand get clearance.

I would also suggest you go with your construction manager to purchase materials. If you can't, make sure you get receipts for everything. You should also be diligent and visit various construction places so you have an idea of what building materials actually cost. That way, if your construction foreman gives you a Price Bill of Quantities breakdown of material costs (e.g., bags of cement, iron rods, cement blocks, etc.), you can challenge things that appear inflated.

I also recommend that you be proactive and shop for your own toilets, sinks, lighting, tile, doors, windows, railing (for stairs and balconies if applicable), garage door/motor supplier, etc. Get 2-3 quotes from places that have the type of household amenities you want for the price range that suits your budget. Otherwise, the construction foreman will take it upon himself to contract this out and the costs will be significantly higher and or the quality may not be to your liking.

For instance you may want U.S. or European standard windows. Those would be single or double pane encasement windows, which cost a bit more but or well worth it. Otherwise, you can go with the standard here which are sliding windows. Depending who you purchase the sliding windows from, they may be subpar and over time do not lock well. They also do nothing for blocking out sound.

To keep costs down, you can do a mix of encasement and quality sliders. You can also elect to have tint put on your windows choosing from available colors. I also do not recommend going with cheap pressed wood doors (solid wood doors are fine for interior rooms) or counter tops as Ghana is a tropical country and over time the humidity and heat will warp your doors and cave in your counter tops. Elect medal doors for your exterior locations and ask if the door's finish is weather proofed before purchase.

Here are a few building tips that will be useful to you getting started.

Tip #1. When you contact someone (or inform your construction manager) to get your land cleared, inform them that you want the quote to be for a set timeframe agreed to accomplish the job.

If you do not do this, you will be paying to have your land cleared by the day and you know what that means. Oh, you don't? Well now, what this means is that the contractor hired to clear your land may drag the process out for days since you elected to pay by the day. If you set an upfront price for total cost regardless of how many days it will take to clear the property you will not incur additional costs day after day, after day. Get the picture? The contractor will want to complete the job as soon as possible so he can move on to his next paying job.

How You Living? | 53

Tip #2. If you can afford it, get a solar water heater tank and put it on top of your house to supply your warm and hot water for bathing and cleaning.

You want it on top of your house to get max sun. It is a waste of money and power to get multiple tankless water heaters installed throughout your home. Especially if in the future, you elect to go solar power for your entire home. All those tankless instant water heaters installed throughout your house for warm/hot water will drive your solar power demand through the roof!

Also, if you go the solar route, ensure your solar inverters are connected to each other when installed. Do not let them tell you they can't be connected. You just have to purchase a card (must be imported from China via Alibaba Express) that is placed under the inverter. That way the system works as one inverter for maximum output. If both your inverters are not needed (don't need a large power output during certain hours/days), you can turn it off with no issues.

You will have one main master unit inverter and one so-called "slave unit" that will keep producing. Just ensure the solar inverters you purchase can be card enabled. You can purchase a 12v, 24v or 48v and that determines the amount of batteries and the arrangement you have to set your batteries up in. The more batteries you have the less your batteries will deplete.

Your inverter will constantly be reading your battery life. The inverter converts DC to AC volts. DC comes from a battery or solar panel and converts it to AC (that which you plug into the wall). The advantage of having the higher voltage is the size of wire you will have to use between the battery and the panel. A higher voltage means you can use smaller wire and this saves money as copper (imbedded in your wires) is not cheap. So plan wisely or your batteries will constantly deplete fast and will not last their total lifespan (typically 5 years).

For instance, a 5-year battery will only last 3 years if you constantly deplete it. If you have workers come on your land to work on your property or house for any reason, MAKE THEM USE A GENERATOR, and not your solar system power! If they use your solar system, it will wear out your batteries quickly and batteries are expensive. A typical solar battery costs $2500 GHC/$430 USD (200 AMPS/12V) and last 5 years.

You can also use windmills to help charge your batteries even if it's a cloudy day. Yes, my potential Ghanaian residents, there is always a fix! We just have to find ways to work economically and environmentally smarter not harder.

Consequently, how does one determine how many inverters a house will need? That depends on the wattage you will be using. You will need to determine the size house you will be building and ALL the wattage potentially utilized. It is safe to buy two. If you will be building a pretty big home; let's just say 3700+ square feet full of electronics, appliances and ceiling fans with lights; I would recommend a minimum of three inverters.

Tip #3. If going the solar route immediately or in the future, remember to use your washer/dryer, devices with pumps, etc., during the day while the sun is up, which means your batteries will not be working hard due to the abundant sunlight.

Okay, that's enough about solar. You are now smart enough to be slightly dangerous.

You don't want to run your washer/dryer, stove and unnecessary electronics at night. Remember, you will have constant appliances running (e.g., fridge, deep freezer, any AC units) so you will have to plan accordingly.

Obtain a Building Permit to Build a Home or Business Structure.

Ideally you want to do this before you break ground. If you don't and you get caught, the Lands Commission will halt your building process and fine you. If you are the risk taking type, and you are able to get your home built without getting caught you may still run into issues down the road.

In Ghana, if the country decides to purchase a large chunk of land where some homes are for whatever reason (i.e., natural resources found, etc.), and they approach you to purchase the land and you cannot produce the building permit you used to build, they do not have to pay you for your property.

To add salt to your wounds, you will also be hit with a hefty fine for having built your home without a permit. This is definitely one of those times when it pays to follow the rules.

All you need is your receipt showing that you have applied for and paid for your building permit. Your foreman will keep a copy with him in case the "Permit Poo Poo" shows up on your property during the building process. Now on to how you obtain a building permit.

1. Conduct research at Lands Commission, purchase your property and submit documentation to the Lands Commission for land Title and Registration. Upon land purchase you should be given an indenture and land survey. You will need copies of these for your permit.
2. Obtain a soil test on your land.
3. Work with an Architect to develop house plan. He/she will provide 4 completed to scale drawings with his/her signature/stamp.
4. If your structure is two stories or more, must meet with a Structural Engineer to validate soundness of house plan. Structural Engineer will lay in his/her study to the Architect's plans with stamp of approval on all copies
5. Obtain topography study on the land
6. Obtain an Environmental Study from the Environmental Protection Agency (EPA) - 1 copy
7. Obtain fire and hydrological report (if requested) - 3 copies
8. Obtain Traffic Impact Assessment (T.I.A) - 3 copies
9. Mechanical or Services Drawing - 4 copies
10. Obtain Geotechnical Report Structural Integrity Report - 3 copies
11. Obtain your land's property rate (these are taxes paid annually, which they do allow to be paid in 12

installments if requested. Your property rate will depend on various factors to include the size of your home. If you don't agree with your evaluated rate, you can request reevaluation.

12. Complete Building Permit Application form (obtain from Lands Commission) - 1 copy

13. Submit all of the above with listed number of copies, as well as 1 copy of your Title Search, 1 copy of your Indenture or Deed or 1 copy of your Land Title Certificate to the Accra Metropolitan Assembly (AMA) Physical Planning Department.

14. Pay the application and processing fees. Additional fee applies but will be calculated based on calculations derived from your submitted structural drawings.

Resource:

For more information visit the AMA website, https://www.ama.gov.gh/building-permit.php

If you have a Construction Project Planner/Manager and a Project Foreman, on your behalf, they will obtain your soil test, topography, fire and hydrological report, T.I.A, and Environmental Study.

Don't want to go through this process? If being in a gated community with barely any property of your own is more your speed, then you can contact the various developers who build apartments, condos and homes on their communities' small plots. They do all the work, you pick your plan, upgrades and colors just like in the West.

Don't expect a much cheaper price as the neighborhoods come with many amenities you are accustomed to, e.g., all paved roads, sidewalks, parks, other recreational areas, and easy access to all the hip and happening stores, restaurants and other businesses.

Regardless of where one choses to live, people here elect to put up walled fences topped with bobbed wire or electrical wire to ward off thieves. Now I know what you must be thinking in your Westernized bourgeoisie inner voice, "Oh my gosh! Like, I don't want to live anywhere that I have to like, be behind bobbed wi-re! Are you like, kidding me?!"

To that sentiment I say that the bobbed wired fences are no different than living in the West with our fancy house alarm systems and hi-tech cameras all over our houses. The alarm systems and security cameras serve the same purpose as a wall with bobbed wire. You just don't see them. I'm just keeping it real.

You definitely need to know how to get around in Ghana. So mosey on over to chapter 4.

Chapter 4

Transportation

There are various ways to get around Ghana. Choose from the trotro, call a Bolt, an Uber or taxi, hire a personal driver for the day or month, and then there is always the option of obtaining and driving your own personal vehicle.

A trotro is a minibus that runs constantly all over Ghana.

Resource

Here's a handy dandy app for you, https://ghtrotro.com/

Information about the app:
https://www.youtube.com/watch?v=p3EqEDNYRYM

The app is also available for download via Google Play Store. Don't be scared off by the crazy guy on the trotro with his head and one arm out the window constantly yelling at everyone on the street. He's not crazy. He is simply trying to increase business by yelling for everyone to get on board and ride the trotro.

If you plan on driving in Ghana, make sure you get your International Driver's Permit before your big move. You can obtain your International Driver's Permit via AAA. It doesn't cost much and can be obtained by completing the application on line and mailing it in with payment and two passport photos.

Pending your state's rules, you can either pick it up or provide a stamped return envelope with mail in application, and they will mail your final document to you. The permit is only good for one year so when applying for it, list the date of effectiveness on the application as your date of travel. You will want to apply for a Ghana driver's license before your International Driver's Permit expires. Keep in mind that obtaining a Ghana license once applied for typically takes up to 1½ to 3 months. Also, on the date of application, you must still have at least 2 months remaining on your Work/Residence Permit.

If you import a vehicle, prepare to pay hefty custom's fees. However, sometimes it may be more cost effective to pay the high fees instead of purchasing on this end. All the ends and outs on this topic is another book all its own. Be conscious about the car you intend to import. If you plan on living in a rural or mountainous area, you will need a 4x4 that doesn't sit too low on the ground. In this instance, shipping your fancy sedan will be a waste of time.

On the other hand, if you will be living in the suburbs or in the heart of Accra, a sedan is sufficient. In addition, before shipping a car to Ghana or purchasing one once in Ghana, you want to ensure that you can actually obtain parts for the vehicle when you need maintenance and repairs.

Lastly, don't forget to purchase car insurance once you buy the vehicle. You will need proof of insurance to register your vehicle. Insurance can be purchased at the DVLA from various insurance companies.

REGISTERING A VEHICLE

To register your imported vehicle you go to the Driver and Vehicle Licensing Authority (DVLA) in your region and do the following:

1. Take vehicle to the DVLA for custom's clearance and identity check.
2. Present the vehicle to DVLA Vehicle Test Station for inspection.
3. If vehicle passes, DVLA Officer will generate an invoice for your vehicle.
4. Pay the invoice fee at the DVLA.
5. Obtain bio-metric capture at DVLA
6. You will be issued new vehicle registration documentation, and a number plate (Also known as license plate)

If you purchase a vehicle once in Ghana, you will follow the Change of Ownership process. You will be able to skip number 1 above if you buy a used car that has cleared customs. You will just need the car's Customs Duties paperwork, which shows that the vehicle has already cleared customs via the car's previous owner or car dealer.

PROCESS FOR CHANGE OF OWNERSHIP

You will need to bring the following:

- A. Application Letter of Transfer. This letter shows transfer of ownership from the owner (or dealer) to you.
- B. Identification Card for both seller and buyer
- C. Two recent color passport photos.
- D. Forms C and VRC (you must obtain form C from the owner)
- E. Approved Roadworthiness Certificate (obtain at DVLA)

1. Obtain and sign all required forms (e.g., Form C & VRC), and attach your pics to the form and submit for processing. The seller's pics should already be on file. These forms can be obtained online via the DVLA website. Form C is your Custom's transfer form. The VRC is the actual Vehicle Registration Certificate (Also known as Change of Car Ownership). Since in this case, the vehicle is not new and has been previously owned, it should already have a vehicle registration number assigned. You will use this information to complete the VRC form which requires information such as the model, color etc.

If you elect to obtain the Form C (if car is not registered, meaning the customs duties have not been paid by the owner, and you will have to pay them) and the VRC form online, you will first need to access the E-services Government of Ghana Service Portal. Once on the portal you will navigate to the downloadable forms section and pay the service fee, and generate an invoice. You will then be able to complete the forms and submit them to the DVLA for processing. Do not forget to attach your two passport size photos as required.

2. Present at the DVLA, the transfer letter. Ensure the transfer letter (to be written by the dealer/owner) clearly states the intention to transfer ownership of the vehicle to you with a description of the said vehicle and monies paid. The letter should also include personal detail for both the owner and yourself (i.e., full name, address). Lastly, the letter should request that the DVLA office concerned provide the required assistance for car change of ownership process.

Once DVLA has validated and processed all documentation filled out by the owner and yourself, you will proceed to step 3.

3. Present vehicle for inspection.
4. If approved, obtain invoice, road worthiness certificate and take to proper DVLA official for final processing and payment of all remaining fees.
5. Receive vehicle roadworthy sticker and all new documentation registered in your name.

Some of these initial steps may be done completely on-line via the online DVLA portal if the website is up and running. https://online.dvla.gov.gh/sign_in

If you are going through a car dealer, and the dealer is doing the transfer of ownership registration on your behalf, you will have to sign documentation giving him Power of Attorney to do so. If it will make you feel more comfortable, insist the transfer of funds be done at the DVLA. That way if you have any issues during the registration process, the current vehicle owner can assist with any clarification needed. The DVLA website states that the owner must be present, however this is not the case. Just make sure you obtain all of the car's documentation as well as transfer letter from the vehicle's owner. In addition, if the DVLA is not too busy on day of purchase, the seller and buyer may take all documentation and applicable photos/fees to the DVLA and have the transfer completed the same day.

Please make sure to ascertain that the seller is the actual owner of the vehicle, meaning his/her ID will match the name on the paperwork! Often times, the person presenting the vehicle for sale may be a friend or relative of the true owner. You want to ensure that you confirm a price with the true owner and do no exchange of money until you can see and place hands on all documentation.

Typical fees as of June 2021 for private (not commercial) motor vehicles:

- Form C: $2.50 GHC
- Form VRC: $2.50 GHC

Road Worthiness Fee: depends on Test Station utilized typical $92-$100 GHC (pending engine size)

Vehicle Registration: $544 GHC (above 2000 cc)

Vehicle Registration: $419.50 GHC (up to 2000 cc)

Truck Registration: depends on cargo tonnage ability.

Other fees required but are not DVLA published are Transfer fee, Service Fee, and Amendment of Registration Fee.

Some lingo on the form that you need to be aware of as the information is used to determine overall registration cost:

Vehicle Type = the engine size (e.g., 2000 cc) and its use (private use or commercial use)

cc (cubic centimeter) = engine size

While you are out and about driving around and running errands or simply enjoying yourself, please be mindful of those on motorcycles and scooters. They will come out of nowhere, not obeying traffic rules, weaving through traffic on your left or right. They usually blow their horn as they are coming through, many of whom are delivery drivers in a mad dash to make their deliveries.

Happy trails!

Chapter 5

Nourishment

Mangoes, plantains, and yams, oh my! Where are you going to get yours, a grocery store or a local market? There are no Big Box grocers so get over it.

Ghana has plenty of grocery stores for your food shopping pleasure. However because there are no Big Box grocers here, that means you will not find everything you like or want at one single grocery store. You will have to put in the time and go to at least two of your favorites. I can only speak for Accra, its outskirts, and main Kumasi areas when I say that the grocery stores do take debit and credit cards. They also have discount cards for frequent shoppers.

Already missing that fav Big Box store you have grown accustomed to? Don't sweat it. None of us should be eating a lot of GMO processed, dyed or bleached foods anyway. Go to the local Ghana market in your area and purchase your fresh fruit, veggies, beans, rice, big yams, cassava, etc. While you are there, you can check out all the other interesting products up for sale. Go as early as you can because parking is brutal!

Oh my goodness! I hear somebody whining over the loss of the processed crap they may not be able to get here in Ghana. Well, truth be told, you will be able to find small "American stores" throughout Ghana. Just ask your driver to spot you one. You may be able to find your favorite toilet paper, cookies, cereal, seasonings, etc.

How do I know? Cause I purchase a few things now and then. Hey, don't judge me! I'm working on cutting back. After all, it's a progression, and I am progressing.

You will also be able to find some of your favorite seasonings at the grocery stores and many more you are going to want to try at the markets.

On a side note, sadly the grocery stores are typically not owned or ran by Ghanaians or other Africans. If you are at one of the grocery stores and filthy (and I mean really filthy) music starts being played, go to the manager and ask him if he would play that mess around his wife or children? He will promptly change it. So infuriating! These owners and managers would not play that filth in their home countries, but they come over to Ghana and blast that crap like it's okay! You let them know it is absolutely not okay! Only then will they stop playing it.

Deep breath, deep breath...find my center.
Okay, moving on.

Vegans, look away for a moment. I have to tell you about the eggs here... they are delicious! You know how if you want a fluffy omelet or some scrambled eggs you have to add a little milk to it? You don't have to add the milk here. They just automatically fluff so beautifully!

Also, because they don't scrub the eggs to death as soon as they come out of the chicken, the eggs last longer outside of the fridge.

Tell you another funny story... I forgot to pick up eggs while at a grocery store. So we were driving home and my brother spotted a vendor on the side of the road selling eggs. He asked me if I wanted him to stop so I could get eggs. In a huff, I said, "I can't buy and eat those eggs. They've been sitting in the sun all day. Are you trying to kill me?!" He started rolling with laughter.

When he finally stopped laughing he told me that the eggs are perfectly fine and assured me that I would certainly not die. I looked at him side-eyed and stated, "I'll buy them, but if I die, it'll be all your fault." Needless to say, I am still alive and well. I did however place my eggs in the fridge as soon as I got home. Like I said, it's a progression.

One market you want to be cautious about is the Agbogbloshie Market. This market itself is just like any other—full of hard working folks trying to earn a living. However, this particular market is located right next to an e-waste dump. The e-waste dump is one of the world's largest dumping grounds for e-waste discarded by the West, mostly from the U.S. and Western Europe.

The workers strip valuable components from old electronics, cables and appliances. They also burn the materials where toxic blooms stifle the air. As the air, food and livestock are affected by these toxins, it would be wise for health reasons, to consider avoiding this market.

The country has recently began relocating traders from the congested, toxic Agboblosie Market to the Adjen Kotoku Market. Ghana is also trying to make strides in getting e-waste and its hazards under control. In 2018, Ghana became the first African country to establish guidelines for sustainable e-waste recycling management and has made small strides in efforts to lessen pollution, with continued efforts unfolding.

Chapter 6

Shipped Goods & Clearing Customs: Recommended Do's and Don'ts of Household Import

Coming from the school of hard knocks when moving to Ghana, some things are just better left in the West. Bringing everything but the kitchen sink is just not worth the headache. If you have special equipment, I certainly advise that you ship it.

Other things I suggest as import worthy are your washer, keep sake furniture or antiques passed down from elders, your favorite small blender, pictures (that you can't scan and reprint) rare books, and herbs in bulk (if you are an herb junkie like myself).

I suggest the washer because those sold here are of lesser quality. They do have Whirlpool, but you are going to pay dearly for this brand here. When it comes to dryers, the quality of dryers in the U.S. is by far superior to those found here, but you will not be able to find a step down that can support the current. I do suggest you purchase a condenser dryer once in country, of all things in such a hot, sunny place because although you will not use it regularly, dryers are useful in retightening underclothes and socks, as well as removing lint off of clothing and towels. It will also come in handy during the peak of rain season.

If you love specialty herbs and use them to make your own teas and tinctures, ship yourself some in bulk. I have only been able to find small quantities being sold and others I have yet to find. Certain oils are also hard to find in larger sizes, such as frankincense and Black Seed Oil. Your favorite small blender is recommended for smoothie, quick chop jobs, making fine grain flours and confection sugar, etc. You may not be able to find your favorite small blender that gets it all done for you fast without having to pull out a large bulky blender or food processor you may not be in the mood to handle or clean afterwards.

For any of you in love with the NutriBullet like I am, don't leave country without it! I have yet to find one in any store. They are impossible to find and the ones being sold here are China counterfeit. They are not made well and do not blend as well—we are talking "itty bitty" blending power. You will not be happy with your product at all unless you are just looking to make smoothies from unfrozen fruit.

I had one I cherished and used for many, many years which I purchased in the U.S. It was so old and used up, that it finally crapped out shortly before I relocated to Ghana. I thought I would just be able to buy another one out of a store once I arrived in country, but was sadly disappointed. Reluctantly, I purchased another brand. Unhappy with the blender I purchased, I sought a NutriBullet from a market vendor.

China has flooded the market with counterfeit NutriBullets here. Yes, China manufactures the U.S. NutriBullet (like most everything else). However, China must make the U.S. NutriBullet product to U.S. specifications. The counterfeit one being sold here is not worth your money.

How can you tell on sight that you are about to "get got"?

Well, let me tell you, the fake Bullet has plastic on the underside of the blade tops, not metal. It also doesn't say made in China on the bottom of the blender, nor does it have the manufacturer information on the underside of the main blender.

Another big tell is that if you rub your finger across the letters on the blender they will easily rub off and there will not be a trade mark ® beside the name on the front of the blender. Sniff...sniff... yes, I got duped. Don't let this happen to you. If the seller will not let you open the box to examine the blender, walk away.

If you import any of your household goods it usually takes 28-30 days to arrive in port. Plan appropriately so you arrive in country before your items do. You will need to make a list of everything you are shipping with its value. Ensure you depreciate for age. This is easiest to create using an Excel spreadsheet. Keep it simple, yet detailed for fast processing.

For example:

	Shipper Name:			Origination Port:	
				Destination Port:	Tema
	Package ID:	Package Type:	Description		Value
1	71	Plastic Tote	Sm Beige bin - Used Women's Clothing; Shirts, Skirts		$200.00
2	1	Box	Family Pictures		$50.00

In the above example, you are the shipper. The package ID is how you have marked the box or tote. Your origination port will be where your container was loaded. This is not where you loaded your things on the container but the port your driver will be delivering your container for transport.

Having your things shipped to Ghana is an easy process. You just locate a shipping company that transports to Ghana. You will not actually be speaking to the shipping company when you call the number listed for a particular company; you will be speaking to the company's Freight Forwarder.

The Freight Forwarder works on behalf of the shipping company to make all of your necessary shipping arrangements. You will be asked what you are shipping (i.e., household goods and or a vehicle), and for an in country (Ghana) address and a contact name/number (if you are not the one receiving on the other end). If you give the Freight Forwarder the information of another person as contact, only that person can obtain your goods. If you have the paperwork, the Clearing Agent will let you go through the red tape clearing.

However, the agent will still need to contact the person on your shipping documentation and get him/her to text them a sufficient photo ID. If you will be acquiring your goods yourself, use your own name and the address where you will be staying. The shipping company's Freight Forwarder will also ask you if you have a Clearing Agent (discussed below).

There are no long term storage facilities in Ghana so you will need to have rented a place to which your goods will be delivered. Do what you like, however, I would not ship any household goods in the same container as a car. If you ship your car in the same container as your household goods and your household goods are cleared by customs but your car is not, you may not be able to clear your container.

I elected not to import a car as it was not conducive to where I choose to live nor did I want to pay high import fees on the vehicle. It would be like paying for the vehicle a second time. No thanks! There are instances in which it does pay to import a vehicle and pay the high fees as costs may end up being less than what you would pay for the vehicle in Ghana. If not, sell the vehicle and bring the cash.

If you are considering selling your home and your items will be placed in a storage facility until you ship them, try and store them in a facility that has a shipping and receiving dock area. It will be easier for you to get your things onto the container as they usually do not bring the container and place it on the ground. It remains on the truck and the container does not have a lift.

You will arrange for your shipping container and driver (person that will deliver the container to you and transport it to the port once loaded), which is usually done through the shipping company Freight Forwarder and are separate fees (a 20- or 40-feet, regular or high cube container pending your needs).

The Freight Forwarder will tell you when the shipping company's next shipping date is. Get two or three quotes from different shipping companies that will pick up from your area (much easier if you live on the East or west coast in the U.S.). You also want to ask them if the containers they use are sea worthy. You may have the option to buy the container otherwise you will just be renting it. If you are renting the container you are going to want to get your goods delivered to you as soon as they clear Ghana customs or you will incur a daily upcharge until the company gets their container back. Don't forget to arrange for friends or a moving company to load your goods on the container. This is not handled by the Freight Forwarder. He/she just ensures the container arrives via the arranged truck driver wherever you need it delivered for loading.

You usually have so many hours to 1 day (overnight if you are lucky) to load all your things onto the container. If you go over your allotted time, you will rack up additional costs. Try not to cut it close, i.e., booking your container only a day before it has to depart from port as this leaves you no time to get your container loaded if things do not go smoothly (e.g., your movers don't show up, or it takes a longer time to load).

Also take into consideration travel time for your driver if you do not live close to the designated port. Do not lose your documentation given to you by the shipping company or the driver of your container. Be sure to ask your Freight Forwarder or container truck driver for the container code and website you may utilize to track your container. If you do ship a container or barrel(s), upon arriving in country make sure you obtain a Passenger's Unaccompanied Baggage Declaration (PUBD) Form before leaving the inside of the airport. This form will be required to clear Customs once your container arrives in country. When you fill out your PUBD Form, the value you state should match the total value of the listing of all your shipped items.

While you are awaiting your container to arrive at the Tema Port in Ghana, unless you know someone who knows someone who is a Clearing Agent, you will need to obtain one. When booking your container for Ghana shipment, you may ask your shipping company's Freight Forwarder if they have a listing of Ghana Clearing Agents they use. You will not actually go to the Tema Port yourself to clear your goods. Instead, you contact your Clearing Agent. If you don't have one already, you will locate a Customs Clearing Agent (also called a Customs House Agent) at the Ghana Revenue Authority (GRA) on the Airport Bypass Road in Accra (in back of the Accra Airport) who will clear your container or barrel(s) on your behalf.

You may also just do a simple internet search for Ghana Clearing Agents. If you bypass these three options (i.e., your initial Freight Forwarder's listing, GRA, internet search), there are other companies on the Airport Bypass Road just past the GRA that are licensed to perform the same service. When you arrive at the gate, they will all be chopping at the bit to be of your service. Just be mindful that not all who pose as performing a certain service is legit.

Whoever you elect as your agent, provide him/her with the required documentation. Also give your agent a hard or soft copy of your shipped items listing with costs. That way they can start working on your customs forms to speed things along before your container arrives.

You use your handy dandy container tracker or you are informed by your Clearing Agent that your container has arrived in port. What in the world do you do now? What you don't do is go to the port, pay and get your things delivered the same day. What book have you been reading? Haven't I already informed you that things don't go at warp speed here like in the West? So just calm your happy self down, because it will be about 5-7 days before your things completely clear customs.

First off, your Clearing Agent will work on your behalf to determine all fees to be paid. Your agent will call you with a required USD amount, and email or text you all the fee documentation to review. If you feel it is unfair, say so. Ask why the cost is set at the amount it is. Your agent will work on your behalf to clarify any issues.

For instance, if Customs says you are being charged for brand new furniture (I didn't tell you to ship any furniture except your precious ancestral antiques) and it is not new, fight back. Many times a manufacture sticker may still be on the underside of your furniture to prove the date of manufacture. You shouldn't be charged a markup simply because you take good care of your things.

Once all the back and forth of disagreement is completed, your agent will send you the final fee documents. The two of you will arrange a meeting date/time for you to hand over your fee money. The Agent will explain the process to you once more, explaining what fee goes to what department, as he knows you have no idea how things work. If you don't know your agent, which most people do not, inform the agent ahead of time that you will require a receipt for your given funds. If you don't, hopefully he will take the funds, pay all the fees on your behalf and then send you a final receipt—this includes your agent's fee.

This meeting will take place in a secured gated area on Airport Bypass Road where many Clearing Agents are located. Once the agent has paid all the fees, usually the same day if you met early enough or the next day, customs will provide your agent with a container release date/time. The container will be delivered to your place of residence. You must have your own personnel to offload your container. If you do not, your agent may be able to arrange a crew, for a fee, to offload your items. Remember, your container will not have a lift gate when you load or unload it.

In the West, when you have your items loaded on your container in your home country, you can contract a lift truck (pay is usually by the hour) to help with the load of your heavier items (if your moving company doesn't have one). In Ghana, the people are very strong and resilient. They don't need special equipment to unload your container, they just "get 'er done."

Have bottled water on hand for your movers and do not pay the driver who delivers your container. That cost was already included when you arranged with your Clearing Agent to have your container delivered to your place of residence. You can provide him a tip if you desire to do so. If there are any issues, do not argue with the driver. Simply give your agent a call, explain the situation and have him speak to your driver. Once your container has been emptied inform your agent promptly, with that done, the task of getting your things into and unloaded at your door has been accomplished.

This is for all the lady readers. Ladies, bring your shoes, underclothes and handbags but please leave the majority of your clothes behind! There is so much clothing and many beautiful fabrics to choose from, you are not going to want to be bogged down with your old western wardrobe. Whether you choose to pick off the rack, bargain at the market, or select from all the amazing fabrics and have your wardrobe custom made (matching headscarf optional), you will be delighted at the comfort and style of the local designs.

Documents you will need to clear your goods: all shipping documents, TIN, valid ID, PUBD Form. If you do not have a TIN yet, use your driver's license or a Non-Citizen National ID number (if already obtained). You will also need enough cash (USD) to pay all the customs fees and your shipper.

If you do not have enough cash, you will have to make up the difference in the local currency (GHC). That means a trip to the ATM (you don't have a bank account yet), and pending what your fees are, that's a lot of GHC to withdraw. For your convenience and theirs, (because they want their fees paid) there are ATMs in the clearing area. If you know you do not have enough cash, go to an ATM that dispenses $2000 GHC at a time so it doesn't take as long, prior to meeting your clearing agent.

Container Tips:

1. Have your container loaded all the way to the top (heavier items on the bottom of course), versus only at shoulder height. Stack it as high as possible for less shifting during transport.

2. If importing any furniture, remove and wrap any glass table tops separately. Use bubble wrap to protect the legs/feet of furniture, as well as tops and corners of table tops, dressers, headboards, etc. If you run out of bubble wrap clothing, towels and old blankets also work well.

3. Purchase a large cargo bar (a heavy duty, steel tube/ with rubber feet), also known as a shoring bar. They cost anywhere from $25-$70 USD pending where you purchase. Once your container is loaded, you will use this bar to brace your goods so they don't shift during transit.

4. Purchase a good lock for your container. Don't use your favorite lock as customs will break the lock for inspection.

5. Don't forget to ask your driver for the shipping code and the website you can use to track your container. Scan/upload, then hand carry via your carryon bag the hard copy of your shipping documents just in case your airport checked luggage gets lost or damaged.

6. Don't be surprised if your container's arrival date begins at under 30 days and then changes day by day to 30+ due to holidays or a longer stay at a certain port along the way. No worries, your container will arrive in due time. So, relax, go have a mango smoothie, some Jollof or Fried rice, or both, with some grilled chicken and yam chips. Or, perhaps some lite soup with goat and fufu. It's all good! Oh my, all this talk about food is making me hungry.

I'm "gonna" break for lunch, and we'll continue in Chapter 7 with information on electronic goods.

Chapter 7

Electronic vs. Electric - What?

When it comes to electronics, you may be a little nervous and anxious concerning what items to bring and which to sell or give away. You may even be considering stocking up on all your favorite items that perhaps you may not be able to purchase in Ghana. That's wonderful and great foresight for planning purposes because American electronic goods are hard to find in Ghana, and what you can find is often extremely expensive.

Before you go running all over town buying up the world, first consider for your stay in Ghana, what your electronic or electrical needs and wants are. I am going to provide you with some information that will make your electronic/electrical transition much smoother.

Note the below contains detailed descriptions about certain items but do not list brand names. This is done on purpose, so as not to sway your opinion about a particular brand item. One person's experience with an item may be great and another person may have had a horrible experience. I simply provide features about and discuss particular items, and hopefully you'll then be able to locate exactly what you need based on your budget and preference.

Many people believe that the terms electronic and electrical mean the same thing and can be used interchangeably. This is incorrect and going forward, it is vital to understand the difference between the two in order to make appropriate decisions about your electrical and electronic needs.

Let me clarify what electronic and electrical means in terms of devices. In general, electronic devices are those which operate on low DC (Direct Current) voltage. These devices usually contain buttons, displays, LEDs, batteries, and circuit boards with microprocessors—an electronic device that is the brain which controls user interaction and actual output—to handle user interactions.

Some electronic devices can take a high AC voltage (Alternating Current) from a wall outlet and convert it to a low DC voltage so that all the digital signals on circuit boards can work properly. In general, these items are small, portable, handheld, table top items that are easily broken if mishandled. These are your everyday items that most people use on a regular basis and don't think about them, unless they break and don't work anymore. Examples include your smartphone, smart watch, laptop, tablet, clock, camera, TV, cable/satellite box, video game console, router, stereo, 3D printer, etc.

Electronic items typically control the flow of electrons as they are received from a low powered source like a battery. In contrast, electrical devices generally use high AC voltage from a wall outlet as is, with very little processing, to perform some type of electrical work (i.e., wall energy needed from device you plug into the wall). This is not to say that electrical devices don't contain electronics because they do in modern times. It's just that their primary purpose is to perform some type of work with the electrical energy.

Here are some examples to help clarify: an electrical stove, refrigerator, washing machine, clothes dryer, hot water heater, air conditioner, ceiling fan, light switch, lamp, flat iron, hair dryer, etc.

Now that we have an understanding of the different types of electronic and electrical devices, let's focus on the items you love and just can't bring yourself to part with or the item(s) may be necessary for your future employment.

It will be beneficial if you start by making an assessment of all your electronic/electrical devices and note whether they run on dual voltage and dual frequency. Ghana's stated common outlet voltage is 230V @ 50Hz single phase using Type D (BS 546: 3 round pins w/center being larger) or Type G (BS 1363: 3 rectangular pins) sockets.

The U.S. common outlet voltage is 120V @ 60Hz single phase using Type A (NEMA 1-15: 2 flat prongs w/1 being larger) or Type B (NEMA 5-15: contains same 2 flat prongs from NEMA 1-15, but adds a round ground pin).

Don't get lost in the technical jargon. The BS # and NEMA # is British and American power plug and socket standards that have been adopted for use by many countries. It's provided just for a reference, so you can look it up and find pictures if you choose. The whole point of stating the above is to note the differences and to mention that manufacturers have taken notice and have long begun to make electric devices that run on both 120/240V @ 50/60Hz.

Most often, the internal circuitry of the item auto detects what voltage and frequency it sees and auto adjusts for you. Meaning, no user interaction is needed. However, there are a few exceptions because some older electronic devices have selectable 120/240V slide switches that must be changed before plugging the device into the wall socket. If done wrong, then the power supply circuit will be destroyed. You see these commonly on old desktop tower computers, laser printers, copiers, and electronic test equipment.

Keep in mind that power selection switch labeling was not standardized from manufacturer to manufacturer, so you may see switches labeled as 110/220V, 115/230V, 115/220V, etc. but just know that it means the same thing. Again, your task as a person ready to embark on a new life in another country is to decide what you want to keep and what you need to sell/give away.

Cost-wise, the priority for sorting out the devices you keep should first be, "is it dual voltage/frequency?" Each electric device or its power adapter contains (or should contain - if missing the item could be counterfeit) a label or stamped impression in the plastic case that gives the overall specifications. This label contains information on the item's part number, trademark, manufacturer, warnings, cautions, current (A or Amps), input, and output.

You need to focus in on the word **"Input;"** which represents the AC voltage input (from outlet) that you can safely plug the device into without damaging anything.

Here is an example, "AC100-240V 1.2A 50/60Hz". This means that the electric device operates within the range of 100 to 240 volts on either a 50 or 60 Hertz (a unit defining how many times an AC voltage sine wave completes one cycle) power system and while in use it draws (consumes) 1.2 Amps of current. Pretty simple right?

Now let me confuse you a bit more and point out the fact that the U.S. also uses 240V (sometimes called 220V) for high current devices or high torque applications. Some items are standard to the home (stove/clothes dryer), but most others are not. Some examples of nonstandard 240V items used in homes are welders, drill press, lathe, milling machine, planer, jointer, band saw, table saw, air compressor, press break, laser cutter, and pneumatic punch just to name a few. These items typically belong to DIYers and those friends that just know how to get things done or know how to make anything from scratch.

For further clarification, 220/240V used in the U.S. is NOT the same as the 230/240V volts used in Ghana, the UK, or elsewhere. Why is this? The US takes 2 ground referenced 110/120V leads ((Hot: 120V, Hot: 120V, Neutral: 0V (Not always used), Ground: 0V)) and the sum of the 2 makes 240V. In Ghana and UK there is only 1 ground referenced 230/240v lead (Hot: 240 V, Neutral: 0V, Ground: 0V), so you see they are not identical.

If you have specialized equipment (solder station, test equipment, tools) that you want/need to keep, then you should make it a priority to contact the manufacturer and/or read the technical manual to make sure your item will work on the UK 230/240V standard. Don't worry about the plug because you can adapt (cut and replace) it to work with whatever socket you need.

Lastly, don't even mention Ghana to a manufacturer because they get brain dumb when you talk about so-called "third world countries," even though they are based off of British standards. Therefore, when you contact the manufacturer speak to them in reference to UK standards instead of referencing Ghana. Hopefully this adds some clarity to understanding the differences in voltages and frequencies.

In my humble opinion, I would not even ship a stove or dryer, unless you can get one from Germany or the UK that is rated for 230V (the quality is far superior and the voltage/frequency requirement is the same as Ghana). Dryers are not common in Ghana and descent electric stoves are scarce (gas being predominant). The hardest part to all the madness is reading the labels on all of the electric goods because they are so tiny. This is where you take pictures of the label with your smartphone and zoom in or go find a kid with young eyes to help out. Make the task of determining voltage/frequency and which items to bring a family affair, so the task is not all on one person and everyone learns something in the process.

When electronic/electrical planning for your Ghana stay, break your planning preparation into short-term and long-term categories. The short-term devices to consider are what you will need to function in Ghana right after you touch down and get off the plane, as well as what your needs will be during your hotel stay (i.e., your immediate need devices). The need will be different pending on whether you are traveling alone or with a family. Ask yourself, "When I touch down, will my items charge directly from USB or will I need to plug them into an electric socket? Are my items actually dual voltage, which will allow me to plug them directly into the socket?"

Some examples are, charging your smartphone, camera, hair trimmers/shavers, electric tooth brushes, battery banks, or flashlights. If your items are dual voltage, it is likely your plug will not fit into the wall socket to work your immediate need devices, so I highly advise that you purchase an international travel charger/adapter that is compatible in the 100 - 240V range.

Tip: The most versatile charger/adapter that I still use to this day is the type that has 4 high speed USB sockets, a USB type C 3.0 Amp connection, and 1 main universal AC voltage socket that adapts (using 3 slides) to more than 150 countries with US/EU/AU/UK plugs.

These are sometimes referred to as a "World International Travel Plug Adapter," "Worldwide Travel Adapter," or "All in One World Multi-Function Travel Adapter." Keep in mind that the travel adapter/charger does **NOT** convert the AC wall voltage to 120V (U.S. standard). It merely adapts your electric device's power connector to Ghana's wall socket type and provides 5V output for USB. So please make sure that what you plug into the adapter/charger is dual voltage compatible.

Now let's look at your long term electric device needs. Plan on buying one or two step down transformers that meet your needs. Personally, I suggest you buy more capacity (rated in Watts or Voltage Amps) than you need because you will need extra wattage to account for instant on "in-rush surge current" when you power on your devices. Meaning, when you first plug in and turn on a device, there is a big surge in current and then it settles out.

In addition, more Watts mean that you can use more devices all at the same time. You want to avoid transformers that read, "auto transformer" as this type of transformer is cheap (minimal design), unsafe, and will not serve the widest variety of your needs.

I recommend the 5000 Watt "Heavy Duty Step Up & Down Transformer" that contains 4 American Type B sockets, 2 - 4 EU Universal sockets, and dual circuit breakers (separate breakers for AC 110-120V and AC 220-240V). You want the type that uses a "toroidal" transformer versus the standard "I-E" type.

There are many brands but I settled on and purchased two different ones. I tested (plugged it right into the wall and it automatically switched to 220V) both in the U.S. and all was fine, but when I came to Ghana one of them worked great right out of the box and the other kept tripping the house circuit breaker. The transformer that kept tripping, I discovered has an auto voltage detect feature that wouldn't react fast enough at turn-on and it wasn't happy at all. I ended up having to modify connections to the main internal relay which resolved this minor issue.

It was definitely not what I expected to happen even after I tested both before shipping. To make things simply, and clear for you, just buy the transformer brand that has the "LT" in the model number (or similar quality). The internal build quality, assembly, and choice of wires are good and it is apparent that quality control was practiced during assembly. This type of transformer also utilizes the external 120/240V slide switches, which simplifies things and eliminates any auto detect feature that may not function correctly. Avoid the transformer that has an "ST" in the model number. You'll have the same problem I had and the internal build quality is terrible. In addition the choice of wires is minuscule and underrated.

Tip: Read reviews from major online shopping websites. You can gain a lot of information from just that alone. A note of caution needs to be mentioned here, concerning the amount of Watts a given step down transformer can handle versus what load (how many things you plug in) is applied to it. If your budget is tight, you can go for a smaller wattage type (e.g., 1000, 2000, 3000W), but keep in mind that whatever you plug into it and use at the same time needs to be less than the overall wattage rating of the entire step down plus a safety margin of 25-50%—for turn-on voltage spikes, high current devices, and heat loss in the transformer during normal use.

Also consider that these step down transformers are not really intended to be used with heating devices as they draw (consume) a lot of current at one time and the internal wiring may not be able to handle it. If it's something small such as a soldering iron or hair dryer, and you want to use quickly, then it may not be that big of a deal. Just try to remove all other devices so as not to add to the load. But if you are cooking a meal on a hotplate for hours then that will be a problem.

Below, I have laid out for you examples of how to calculate your total wattage to see if the devices you want to step down will work in Ghana. If an example does not have a calculation beside it, this is typically because the wattage is so low that no additional wattage is required.

These are just rough figures, so verify your exact device's rating from the labels mentioned earlier. You want to look for "Input" Watts (W), Volts, or the Amps (A) used by the device. Don't confuse this with "Output" specifications.

If you see a rating listed in horsepower (HP) then multiple that particular number by 746 to convert it to Watts. If the overall function of the device involves a heavy duty motor that is continuously being used, then also add the 25-50% margin into the calculation. If a label is missing or illegible, then use household solar system sizing calculators (there are many charts online) to estimate the Watts used for various household items.

W + Percent Safety Margin = Total Watts
Volts x Amps = Watts
HP x 746 = Watts
(applies when you have something rated in Horse Power)

Let's walk through the first example together, the good old Rice Cooker!

Rice Cooker is 500W + 25% = 625W
What I'm stating is 25% of 500 is 125.
This is your safety margin.

You must then add the safety margin to the initial watts to obtain total wattage required:
500W + 125 = 625W

You have to add 25% as a safety margin to ensure the device will work and not be underrated in terms of current.

Microwave	1100W + 50% = 1650W
Blender	400W + 25% = 500W
Food processor	600W + 25% = 750W
Stand mixer	1200W + 25% = 1500W
Curling iron	1500W
TV	150W
Video game console	300W
Laser printer/copier	(120V x 6.5A) + 25% = 975W
Washing machine	1000W + 25% (better 50%) = 1250 - 1500W
Vacuum	1200W + 25% = 1500W
Table saw	1800W + 25% (better 50%) = 2250 - 2700W

Volts x Amps = Watts
Utilizing Volts x Amps (A) to obtain required Watts

Cordless drill (charger)	120V x 2.8A = 336W
Drill (corded)	120V x 4A = 480W

Utilizing Horse Power (HP) x 746 constant to obtain required Watts
HP x 746 = Watts

Air Compressor 3 HP (3 x 746) + 25% (better 50%) = 2798 - 3357W

Calculate the total Watts of the items you want to plug into the step down transformer and use at the same time. So if you were cooking and wanted to use the blender, microwave, rice cooker, food processor, and printer/copier at the same time then you need to account for a total 400 + 1650 + 625 + 750 + 975 = 4400W consumed by the step down transformer. You can see that a 5000W step down is ideal because it gives you more options. If you buy a smaller wattage transformer, you will simply have to unplug more devices because you won't be able to use them simultaneously.

Again keep in mind that the step down converts the voltage only and not frequency (Hz), so make sure your device can operate safely on 50/60 Hz. If you own very nice hair clippers that plug into an outlet, you must verify the 50/60 Hz frequency compatibility! Even though you can get the voltage stepped down, the 50Hz frequency in Ghana will NOT work on hair clippers designed for use on 60 Hz power.

Tip: When you get to Ghana, you can buy nice clippers in major retail stores.

Final electrical caution to note is to NOT plug in power strips to expand the number of outlets you want to use. For example, you cannot turn two outlets into twelve by using two power strips. While technically possible, the above wattage considerations MUST be taken in account! Otherwise, this is a recipe for disaster and something will likely go up in smoke.

This concept makes it too easy to plug in a bunch of devices without regard to the total Watts being used. You can overload a home outlet just the same and burn down the whole house. My recommendation is to NOT use power strips with step down transformers.

The last bit of advice I have on step downs is the higher the Watts capability you buy means the unit will be heavier than a smaller one. Just an FYI for shipping considerations, the 5000 Watt units weigh in the 30 lb. range and a 1000 Watt transformer weighs about 13 lbs.

In a long-term rental or permanent living residence, it would behoove you to look into the purchase of a whole house voltage stabilizer—also called automatic voltage regular or AVR. This is a must because the incoming voltage to the house fluctuates a lot in Ghana. I have personally witnessed 190ish - 297V and, yes, devices smoke when this happens. As to why, I cannot say, but take it from someone who lost a media server due to over voltage; don't risk it!

Now for more in-depth understanding on stabilizers, note that there are different types of voltage stabilizers which I will discuss in the order of best quality and availability to least quality.

The first type of stabilizer is a relay type that is supposed to regulate the output voltage in a range of 230 - 240V AC. These generally can be purchased with a rating in the range of 1000 - 5000 Watts, containing a couple of digital displays, and made to sit on the floor.

One generally buys multiple types of these units and places them in each room that contains the electric devices that need protection. This stabilizer monitors the incoming voltage and based on the measurement calculated it opens a relay to maintain the output within the specified range as mentioned above.

You may also see on the rear output panel of some stabilizers an output voltage labeled "110V". If you see this, you may become all excited and think you will not need a step down transformer, which would save you quite a bit of money. Not so fast!

Upon further investigation, the downside is that the "110V" labeled output is ungrounded and doesn't have a third ground pin. This voltage stabilizer also does not regulate all the voltage that it puts out. The main 230 - 240v output is regulated, but the "110V" output is NOT. There is simply a stepped down winding (cuts voltage in half) on the incoming voltage transformer that is ran to the rear output panel. No processing, handling or regulating of the voltage whatsoever.

Let's walk through a simple example of how that "110V" output works on relay type stabilizers. Let's say the input voltage from the power grid in Ghana is stable and the incoming voltage is 230V. This would make the "110V" marked output measure at approximately 115V. If the voltage is a little high, around 250V, then your "110V" marked output will measure approximately 125V.

Likewise, if the input voltage from the power grid is 190V, then your "110V" marked output will measure approximately 95V. Now on a really bad day in Ghana when the power reads 280 - 290V, your "110V" marked output will measure approximately 140 - 145V. By now the problem should be obvious. For your American 115 - 120V only devices, they will let out the smoke in a hurry.

In the techie world, we say all electronic devices contain smoke. The goal is to keep the smoke in. Once you do something crazy like drop a device on the ground, in water or plug/force a cord in the wrong way, then you have now let the smoke out. Your next call would be to your favorite techie buddy who knows all these things and you tell him everything about your device that doesn't work, except what you did to break it. Shame on you.

The exchange would go a little something like this: Techie friend, "What's wrong with your device? What doesn't it do that it normally should do?"

End user, "I don't know. I just tried to use it and it doesn't work anymore. I have no idea what happened to it."

Techie friend, "Can you elaborate?"

End user, "I just turned it on one day and it don't work. Like I said, it's just broke."

Techie friend, "Bring it by tomorrow and I'll look at it."

End user, "Okay, thanks. You're a life saver!"

End user then says to himself, "I sure hope he doesn't find out that I dropped my phone in the toilet."

I have placed a lot of emphasis into describing the relay type of stabilizer because they are the cheapest and are what most people often look to buy. The output accuracy is in the range of 10 - 15% and only available in single phase.

The next type of stabilizer is what's called a servo controlled stabilizer. This is nothing more than an electromechanical variable transformer that is controlled electronically by a microprocessor. This microprocessor is adjusted to regulate the output at a particular set voltage (let's say 230V) and any input fluctuation (high or low) is automatically corrected to maintain the set point. Thus all of your devices connected in your home will be protected.

The output accuracy range is typically 1 - 3%, which is very good, but only has a reaction time in the milliseconds to seconds. In the electronics world, that is creeping around like grandpa. As with any mechanical device you need to keep an eye on it, blow the dust off, and check for any parts that may wear out (in years).

Whole house servo stabilizers can be purchased in either single or 3 phase, with the latter being more costly because three transformers are used vs one for single phase. Each transformer is made with a lot of copper wire and therefore the cost is higher. Output capacities typical of this type range in the 10kW (10,000W) to 500kW. The specifications when looking at higher rated stabilizers will often be stated in kVA (Kilo-volt Amps). Watts and Volt Amps are both a measure of power rating, but keeping this simple let's just say they are the same when shopping for stabilizers.

The last type of voltage stabilizer is called static or IGBT controlled. This type of voltage stabilizer is purely an electronic device using high powered transistors, no moving parts and generally has an output accuracy of 1%. You can consider these to be low to no maintenance (except blow the dust off) and of the three types being the absolute best.

These also can be purchased in either single or 3-phase for whole house distribution. The reaction time to input fluctuations is far superior to the relay and servo types. Static stabilizers also have capacities in the 10kVA to 500kVA range. You can expect to see these used in industrial applications and not commonly found in households due to the high cost.

Loaded with all this information, you may be wondering, Which one do I purchase? The simple answer is this, the one that you can find in Ghana and fits your budget.

The servo and static stabilizers will require the services of an electrician to wire/integrate into your existing or new electric service panel (circuit breaker box). You can find relay and servo stabilizers in all major electronic retail stores in Ghana. The static type is difficult to find and may have to be imported, which means more cost.

For me, a 15kVA servo controlled stabilizer works perfect for my needs. I have found that in an emergency situation where the stabilizer fails, it is easy to buy versions with a bypass switch that will get you back up and running quickly. It's a matter of turning off the stabilizer switch and turning on the bypass switch (both can NOT be on at the same time), which takes all of about 2 - 3 seconds plus your time to get to wherever the stabilizer is located. Just know that everything down the line, throughout your house, will now be unregulated.

If you ship household items, then step down transformers will support your 120V devices that you just can't part with or simply can't or don't want to repurchase once in Ghana. You may have a lot of specialized kitchen tools (stand mixer, food processor, blender, etc.) or expensive power tools (drills, drill press, planer, table saw, miter saw, router, sanders, etc.) that you just can't let go of. Hey, I totally understand.

Just know that shipping these items can be costly as you must declare your electronics when clearing customs. However, it is better to have what you need than to need something and cannot buy it anywhere in Ghana.

I must also caution that there are many items listed on Ghana websites for sale and referenced as name brand, but some are counterfeit knockoffs, as referenced in Chapter 6. In my experience, American, Japanese, British, and German appliances/tools are far superior than the rest.

If you ship your items, know that you do have some options. You can load up all your household items on a 20 ft or 40 ft shipping container, as discussed in chapter 6, or if shipping less items, barrels may be the cheaper route to utilize. Shipping barrels can be either metal, plastic or heavy cardboard type. They have a large clamp or screw lid on the top to allow easy opening of the entire top of the barrel. You simply pack your items that you want shipped in these barrels and have them shipped just like a container. More than likely they will be placed inside of a shipping container to keep them safe and for easy loading/unloading onboard ship.

Keep in mind this is your personal stuff and if something gets broken, the fault is all on you. So pack things extremely well. In fact go overboard (no pun intended), and spare no expense on packing material. If you or your spouse work for an employer that does a lot of shipping/receiving, get the old left over scrap material that's designated to be tossed in the trash. It's free and can save you lots of money.

Whatever you plan on bringing with you take it out of the original box (if it's too bulky) and wrap/protect with bubble wrap and/or heavy duty cardboard.

Be creative. You can even use your clothes or bedding material (sheets, pillows, blankets) as protective material. It's your stuff and it's going to get banged around throughout the shipping process. If you decided to keep it, then it must have some value to you so protect it because some items are very hard to come by in Ghana and cannot be replaced.

As a general rule, when considering what to ship, purchasing appliances in Ghana is cheaper when compared against the dollar. So your everyday items can just be repurchased here and may not be worth the shipping costs and paying customs fees.

If contemplating shipping a TV consider the fact that U.S. TVs contain what's called an ATSC tuner that's made to be used in the United States, Mexico, Canada, and South Korea only. This is where you plug in the cable or antenna line (RG59 or 6 coax) on the back of the TV. ATSC tuners DO NOT work in Ghana. If you still want to ship your beloved TV, then ship it knowing that you will have to buy a DVB-T2, DVB-S2, or DVB-T2/S2 set top converter box. This replaces your tuner on your old TV and you just view the TV content via a HDMI, RGB, or component TV input.

Note that the T2 is the second generation of the terrestrial (OTA - Over The Air) digital television standard. Likewise, S2 represents the second generation of the digital television satellite standard. Depending on your preference, you can opt to purchase a combo box that can tune either satellite and OTA or one of either type. These boxes are hard to find in mainstream stores as the digital switch over from analog TV happened about 5 years ago. They can however be found in the local markets where you can try before you buy. They have power available; just ask them to hook it up.

If you are on the fence as to whether you should sell or ship your American TV(s) and or external DTV/cable converter, my advice would simply be to sell it. I will take my leave from this chapter by informing you that once in country, please purchase some "Universal EU to UK plug adapters" because some home appliances (lamps, fans, clocks, kitchenware, bug zappers, chargers, DTV tuner boxes) sold in Ghana's stores contain only 2 pin type C or type F EU plugs.

You need to be able to adapt them to the UK type G socket. So just buy the Universal UK plug adapters in order to plug the things you purchase "in Ghana" directly into the wall.

Those of you moving from the UK and other countries with the same voltage, frequency, and plug types as Ghana, are in a much better position than those relocating from the U.S. Sometimes that's just how the cookie crumbles.

Chapter 8

Home Country & Ghana Mail

Have you thought about how you will retrieve your home country's mail? You will have final bills to pay. In addition, if a company owes you money and needs to mail you a check where will they mail it? If you do not have a reliable, trustworthy friend or family member, or you just don't want others in your business you need to check out the digital (virtual) mailbox services available to you.

You will want to set this up prior to leaving your home country. Don't forget to also do this for any business you run yourself as well. Find a digital mailbox service that allows you to add more than one person and/or business to your mailbox. Doing so will allow you to have your personal and business mail sent to the same address at the cost of one account.

I suggest changing your address with the post office and sending your mail to your digital mailbox no less than one month prior to your departure date to ensure it is working properly. The US Postal Service requires 14 days notice before they start forwarding your mail to another address. So don't wait until the last minute to fill out and submit the change of address and forwarding forms. Just remember to get all your product ordering in before you change your address to the digital address.

There are some digital mailbox companies that will also ship certain size packages to you in Ghana (for a price). You will just have to have the order sent to the digital mailbox company's regional shipping center address instead of your regular digital address. How digital mailboxes typically work:

Compare options, then select and pay for your plan. Have all required documentation notarized and upload onto the digital mailbox service website.

Next, you need to change your mailing address with the Post Office and whomever you need to. If you were between addresses (in process of selling your home and moved to another location pending the sale), don't forget to forward that address' mail to your digital mailbox address.

You can do a web search and read about all the In's and out's of the various digital mailbox services and prices used online and decide which company and service plan best fits all your specific personal and or business needs. Be sure to check your virtual mail at least once a week as the time limit for viewing your scanned mail may expire.

In reference to your Ghana mailing needs, there is not a lot of mail distributed in Ghana. As Ghanaians are personable people, most business is conducted face to face. That's a plus, because you can say good riddance to daily junk mail!

To have a package delivered to your home or a takeout delivery, you will provide the delivery service your digital address. To locate your digital address you must go to Ghana Post GPS and download the app to your phone via Google play or web version: https://ghanapostgps.com/

After you have downloaded the app, ensure your phone's location button is on. Then open the app and click on the button to view your address.

Resource:

Here is a website that will explain in detail, and walk you through the process step by step if needed: http://urudrive.com/blog/ghana-now-has-a-digital-addressing-system-heres-how-it-works/

Your digital address is also good to know so you can provide it to your driver or use it yourself (if you elect to drive yourself) to get back home until you become familiar with locations and routes. If you need a Post Office box, check out the various locations nearest where you plan on residing.

You can also use digital addresses to locate most businesses in Ghana.
Visit their website at https://ghanapost.com.gh/.

Chapter 9

Obtaining Long-term Residency or Citizenship

If you plan on putting down roots and investing in Ghana, you will need to work towards obtaining long-term residency or Ghanaian citizenship. The quickest route to long term residence is either Indefinite Residence or Right to Abode.

Indefinite Residence Permit. In order to apply for this status, one must first reside in Ghana for 5 years or more or be married to a Ghanaian. I have placed the link below. However, you will not find fees and forms located on this government website.

As stated prior, Ghana is not yet a website, click, click country. The people prefer the personal touch. You must show them who you truly are. Have you proven yourself as a worthy applicant these past 5+ years?

If you have put down roots in Ghana and have contributed to the country or your local community, by this time you will know exactly who to contact for required documentation and required fees. You will also have made wonderful Ghanaian friends who can write you two character letters to submit with your package.

If that doesn't make you feel all warm and fuzzy, then you can just visit the Department of Immigration. Once you believe you have obtained the right to Indefinite Residence, you will need character letters from 2 Ghanaian citizens, your Curriculum Vitae (also known as CV/Resume, see chapter 1) and any other documentation the Department of Immigration requests from you at that time with required fee.

However, this will not be on your horizon for many moons to come.
https://www.mint.gov.gh/services/indefinite-residence-permit/

Right to Abode

This type of permit is usually given to a Ghanaian who has lost his/her citizenship by reason of acquisition of a foreign nationality. However, Right to Abode is also extended to a person to a person of African descent in the Diaspora.

This is as clear as mud and I personally don't know, nor have I heard of anyone who has been able to obtain it. Perhaps it is reserved for extraordinary individuals or those from other African countries living in the Diaspora who wish to return to the continent and abode in Ghana.

The process takes approximately six months. Information on fees, application and required documentation to be given only to those who actually meet the criteria. For more information visit https://www.mint.gov.gh/services/right-of-abode/

Citizenship

Ah the pièce de résistance, the ultimate honor bestowed upon one seeking to reside in Ghana forever! Per the Ghana 2000 Citizen Act, one can obtain either Dual Citizenship or Naturalized Citizenship. Dual citizenship can be bestowed upon a Ghanaian who has obtained citizenship in another country or to anyone else of a foreign country as approved by the President.

In order to be a Naturalized citizen, you must be able to prove that one of your parents or grandparents were Ghanaian born. Yes, according to the 2000 Citizen Act, if you do not have Ghanaian heritage, you cannot apply for full Naturalized Citizenship. Perhaps it may change in the future, but for now obtaining dual citizenship will have to suffice. This is no small feat; one who obtains dual citizenship has truly arrived and should be very proud of the accomplishment.

For most reading this book, Dual Citizenship will apply. So I will speak explicitly on this. Dual Citizenship is also known as Citizenship by Registration. To apply one must reside in Ghana for at least 7 years (if married to a Ghanaian, 5 years), and be of good character. One cannot have a criminal record in home Country.

As of 2021, to apply, the following process is required:

1. Obtain and complete Dual Citizenship Form 10 (500 GHC)
2. Submit 4 passport photos
3. Submit copy of birth certificate
4. Written Application of registration addressed to the Honorable Minister of the Interior stating one's request for Dual Citizenship
5. Good character letter(s)
6. Copy of valid Work and Residence Permit
7. Pay 100 GHC processing fee (may be paid after processing of documentation)[12]

Although not required, if you are or have been a working professional or have obtained and utilized a vital trade, I also recommend including a current CV (Resume).

Once all documentation has been accepted and processed, the average waiting period is one month. Children born in Ghana of foreign parents with no Ghanaian heritage (parents or grandparents), are not given automatic citizenship. However, one who obtains the honor of citizenship can then apply for the citizenship of his/her children. "Ain't dat" nice? Hope you feel better now even though you may have been in your feelings because you found out that you cannot be a Naturalized Citizen.

As of 2021, the fee for dual citizenship application is 500 GHC ($85 USD), processing fee is an additional 100 GHC ($17.50 USD). If you qualify and seek to be a naturalized citizen the fee is 6,000 GHC ($1,039 USD), plus processing fee. As you work towards obtaining citizenship or permanent residency, please do not forget to renew your Work and Residence Permit and Non-Citizen National ID annually prior to the expiration dates.

In addition, ensure you maintain a valid Passport and Visa as you will not be able to renew the required permit and ID with home country documents that are out of date. If you have skipped to this section in haste, please go back and read chapter 1.

This book wouldn't be totally complete nor honest if I did not also inform you about things I personally do not like about Ghana. As such, proceed to chapter 9 and discover the major things that Ghana must improve upon.

Chapter 10

What I Don't Like About Ghana

Ghana is a great country but like all countries, it has room for improvement. I am not going to harp on meaningless minuscule things that have to do with one's personal preference. No, I am going to briefly discuss the top 5 things, in my opinion, Ghana needs to address ASAP.

Please keep in mind that while the issues discussed below are major challenges Ghana must overcome, she is a relatively re*new*ed country that has made great strides since obtaining independence from colonization on March 1957, while still dealing with (like most of Africa) the effects of colonization, (e.g. unjust policies, theft/exploitation of resources and artifacts, etc.) of the leaders (and their affiliates) of other countries/continents.

I say renewed and not new because Ghana was a nation (previously known as Wagadugu and also Ghana Empire) prior to colonization. One does not become "new" simply because a former oppressor redraws its borders and declares it so, as if the nation (regardless of what it was called), and its people had never existed prior to the oppressor's arrival.

1. Bribery

Ghana has a bribery problem that has absolutely nothing to do with taking advantage of one who is a foreigner, this is the everyday norm for all. It is an ugly unspoken taboo that must be addressed. It is so bad that the expectation of a bribe has become ingrained into the culture. To expect and accept a bribe here is an unrighteous norm. On what do I speak? Many people actually expect you to pay them a bribe (which they call "a gift") to do their job (e.g. holding your postal box key hostage, obtaining PUBD form at airport, getting certain major things registered, etc.). No one should have to pay a bribe just for a person to do their freaking job, no matter how small the bribe! This madness needs to stop. Those others look up to, (e.g., government officials, law enforcement, leaders and supervisors of all businesses) need to set an exemplary example. Let the good flow from the top down instead of the bad.

There needs to be a taught and pushed Ghanaian honesty and integrity standard in all one does. This standard should also be mandated and enforced upon ALL foreigners living in and conducting business through, or running a business in Ghana regardless of how much they invest in or loan to the country. Let's do right by one another and strive to build a great nation together.

2. Electricity

Ghana has one of the highest access rates to electricity on the African continent. Ghana passed the Renewable Energy Act 2011 to provide for the management, development, utilization, sustainment and adequate supply of renewable energy.[14] However, the country still suffers from power shortages as well as efforts to keep up with the ever growing demand for electricity. One way Ghana is contemplating resolution of its power shortages, is to build a nuclear power plant as well as renewables.[15]

Many developed countries utilize nuclear power plants for electrical production, with the U.S., France, Japan and China having the largest number of such plants. The use of these power plants is under great debate due to concern over the deployment and safety of the nuclear fission reactors to produce the electricity. Although the risk is low, in the event of accidents or malfunctions the nuclear power is a threat to the environment and people due to risk of radiation exposure.[16]

I'm not a big fan of nuclear power but I am all for hydroelectric power generation, solar power and wind turbines. Ghana currently utilizes hydroelectric generation as a major power source, yet still faces shortages due to fluctuating water levels, high losses in the distribution system, and corruption. Going forward the country seeks to curb these issues via digitalization and grid optimization.[17]

In the meantime, if you just can't deal with power outages invest in a generator for those pesky power outage gaps. If your funds allow, invest in a whole house generator that will switch on seamlessly whenever there is an outage. Or once your home is built/purchased, you can invest in solar.

There are some residential rentals that have generators if you are willing to pay the extra cost in rent. I can honestly say that I haven't experienced extremely long power outages where I currently reside. Therefore I don't have major issues with the power going out in spurts, as I have just planned my life around it.

My concern is for all those in country who will never be able to afford a deep freezer, a generator or solar panels for their homes or small businesses. To lessen the effect of outages, I wash my clothes at night so as to hang them out to dry first thing in the morning (just in case the power is out come morning).

I keep my laptop and phone charged. If my phone goes low, I utilize power packs to recharge them. I keep some frozen water/juice in my freezer and pull them out on extremely hot days to keep cool and drink. I fill and keep 2 larger (e.g. 1 liter size) frozen plastic bottles in my deep freezer to aid it in case of a longer power outage.

I also keep the bulk of perishable food items in a deep freezer (meats, veggies, bread etc.). It would also be beneficial to you if you do your research and invest in a good refrigerator. It will keep your food cold even during reasonable power outages (as long as you keep its doors closed).

What I Don't Like About Ghana | 115

Additionally, your food will stay fresh longer. Some American, Korean (e.g., Samsung), Japanese (Toshiba) as well as Germany's Bruhm models will serve you well. If you go the cheapest route when purchasing your fridge/deep freezer, you will surely regret it. When you go to purchase the appliance (called electricals here) look for a model that has a wide low and high input voltage range.

Typical input rating is 220V to 240V. If you research a brand/model on line and it states it has the capacity to do say 165V-280V (high and low voltage range), that's even better.

What I'm trying to relay to you is that you want to purchase an appliance (fridge/deep freezer) that is capable of handling the high and low swings of voltage, as Ghana's input voltage from its power grid is not stable.

3. Open storm drains /waste management

Most of the streets here do not have covers on their storm drains. I have seen cars tipped up having accidentally driven off the road (not far to go) into one. People fall into them and they are a nuisance at the markets, as you constantly have to watch your step which is not always easy to do in such a crowed location.

People even throw trash into them and trash flows into them as well. This in-turn causes the drains to fill up and when rain season comes water cannot flow from them into gutters, which means unnecessary flooding occurs. Come on Ghana, this may be initially costly but it is an easy fix. Just put iron grates over the storm drains, please!

In reference to waste management, Ghana is doing its part to improve this problem, although more waste recycling plants are needed throughout the country. However, for total waste management to truly work, the citizens of Ghana must do their part and stop carelessly littering, throwing trash haphazardly all over the place.

Let's take pride in Ghana and make her a place of beauty and not a place of filth. Imposing hefty littering fines on those who don't have much is pointless. Perhaps making offenders spend time cleaning littered streets as well as educating the youth on the importance of proper trash disposal would help eliminate this problem.

4. Treatment of the historical (slave trade) Diaspora

On this topic there are no words to express my deep disappointment. Yet, not so much that I'm leaving or wouldn't make the choice to move here all over again.

So, what do I have beef with? The high cost of GIPC "foreigner" business registration ($2852 USD, with a $463 USD every two year renewal), the high cost of initial business registration itself ($2500 USD), and annual fees for required documentation to remain in Ghana legally year after year, after year.

After one's initial year's documentation fees, the continued average annual cost for one's Work/Residence Permit and Non-Citizen ID is $1231 USD per person! It is an unjust slap in the face to constantly charge those whose ancestors were once sold, invite their offspring back home, then charge them outlandish yearly fees to remain in country.

Would not that money be better spent in the establishment of businesses (which creates jobs for others), or purchasing Ghanaian goods in which the money goes directly into the pockets of Ghanaians which fosters economic growth?

If Ghana wants those of the historical Diaspora to invest in Ghana, Ghana must also invest in the Diaspora. Those of the continental Diaspora are clearly treated differently from true foreigners (those not of African bloodline). Why then are the historical Diaspora lumped in with other nations and charged the same fees year after year?

If those of the historical Diaspora are truly the brothers and sisters of Mother Africa, and Ghana welcomes them home, why are they treated no differently than any other typical foreigner when it comes to documentation to remain in Ghana or to register a business and invest via the GIPC? Per a recent discussion I had with the GIPC, the concerns in treatment of those of the historical Diaspora has been heard. As such there are policies for improvement currently in parliament undergoing discussions. The GIPC is doing its due diligence in trying to address the business concerns of the African historical Diaspora.

I just hope the policies it put forth gets through all the typical political red tape. I love Ghana, however, during this "Decade of Return" she must do right by the historical Diaspora so their return is truly a joyous one, and not a burden. Only time will tell. Come on Ghana, make no mistake, the world is watching and those of the Diaspora are rooting for you.

5. The Haves and the Have Nots

The ultimate thing I don't like about Ghana, is the same thing I don't like about the West; **the great divide between the haves and the have nots**. However, the have nots in most developing countries are at a greater disadvantage than those in the West as there are no government housing programs (e.g., Section 8) or food programs (e.g., SNAP, WIC etc.) to help those in need.

Many remote villages live in extreme poverty, most with no running water or electricity. There are a few private companies that are doing their part in helping the needy, but the need is vast. Ghana does not need more "for profit" NGOs. She needs her own manufacturing companies, mega farms, sustainable housing, clean power sources, and clean waste management/recycling initiatives.

Come, develop businesses, create jobs and donate to reputable Non Profit Foundations and organizations who truly seek to help Ghana help Ghana.

Berakah Infinity is a nonprofit foundation that seeks to do its part in alleviating the burden of hunger and accessible drinking water to rural and remote locations. If you or someone you know has been reluctant in the past to donate due to organizations that hoard the bulk of contributions citing "Administrative fees," be reluctant no more.

Resource:

Berakah Infinity donations go directly to projects to help those truly in need. All donations are tax deductible. To learn more and contribute, visit https://berakahinfinity.org

While in Ghana, if you are out and about and have some money or food you wish to give to the children, be mindful on how you do so. If you are coming out of a grocery store and children approach you for food and you have something you wish to share with them, do not give the food item to one child assuming he/she will share with the other children.

Pass out what you have to all the children and keep it moving. If giving small change/bills at a stop light, wait until the light is about to change (you will have to learn the timing cycle). If you don't do this, other children will start to bombard your car and I'm sure you do not have enough to give to the masses. Let alone having to see their little tiny sad faces pressed against your window because you don't have anything left to give them.

I've gone to bed many a night with a heavy heart praying for these beautiful children who need a helping hand. Which is why Berakah Infinity seeks to help as many underserved as possible. If you have it in you to give, please do so.

> *"To whom much is given, much is expected,"*
> — Luke 12:48.

Well, there you have it… the good, the bad and the ugly. It's how I see things. Take it for what it's worth. Once improved upon Ghana will not be great, she will be amazing! Hey, it's been fun.

You've been so kind in lending me your time and eyes while I inform you about the potential place in which you are considering to call home and or perhaps start a business.

If you decide to take the Ghana plunge, in chapter 11, I'll leave you with some extra tips that are sure to come in handy before and after you make the big move.

Chapter 11

Extra Tips

Bank Cards (Debit/Credit) and Checks

Make sure your bank cards are not about to expire soon (within a year or less). If they are contact your bank(s) informing it that you will be residing in Ghana for a while and need to obtain a new card(s).

Also have the bank note your account(s) for you being in Ghana so you don't get your account(s) locked down the first time you use your card(s) in Ghana. If you have a child in college you give a monthly living allowance to, elect to give him/her a student bank/debit card that you can load via e-banking.

When it comes to writing checks (if ever needed), talk with your bank about the ability to write electronic checks. If you ever need to send a check to a loved one etc. ensure your bank allows for adding someone (other than a company for bill paying purposes) to the "Bill Pay" section for a one time electronic check to be sent. After which you can delete that person from Bill Pay.

Documentation

In case your documents (passport, driver's license, birth certificate, etc.) are lost or stolen, always make sure you make and keep copies (to include soft copies) of all your IDs prior to any international travel.

Schooling

If you have children moving to Ghana with you and they are going to school online, they should be able to continue online. However, the child will have to log in (site will probably not allow access unless signing on via VPN) at the same time he/she was required to log on in home country. If you have younger children this may be a huge challenge due to the time difference. Also, if the school gave the child a laptop to utilize and it is mandated that the child only use that particular laptop for classes, once schooling is completed (e.g., high school graduate), you will have to get the laptop back to the school or you will have to pay for it prior to receiving any academic credentials (e.g., official High School Diploma).

Schooling is not the same in Ghana as in the West. Parents have to pay for their children's education here. There are many schools of various status. You will have to take the time to visit the ones in the area you will be living in and ask questions about the curriculum and fees. In the area I reside, one can pay on average $1500 GHC ($262 USD) per semester, with a small discount given for additional children going to the same school. Pending the school, you may have to pay additional monies for books and uniforms.

Bottled Water and Toilet Paper

Ghana is a tropical country so stay hydrated. When you leave your house or apartment take a bottled water with you. If you are going to be running around all day from place to place you may want to invest in a small cooler and pack it with a few water bottles. If you forget your water, you can always opt for some refreshing coconut water that can be found along almost every roadside.

Take a small roll of toilet paper along with you as well. Some businesses are often out of it or do not provide it. As an alternative, invest in some scent free, additive free "expandable wipes." These are much easier to carry around than toilet paper and can be purchased via eBay or Amazon. In addition, if you seek to avoid animal glycerin sources, you should bring a travel size bottle of your own glycerin free soft soap and or hand sanitizer.

Learn Twi

There are many languages spoken in Ghana, to include English and Pigeon. However, Twi is a language spoken by almost everyone. There are some very good YouTube videos as well as a free Twi app (can upgrade for a fee), downloadable via GooglePlay store that are very helpful.

Learning the language will help you immerse in the culture and make a lot of helpful business as well as friendship connections.

Godbox Tours

This is a Ghanaian Pan African interfaith tour agency that showcases the history and culture of Ghana.

Customize your tour or book a workshop.
Visit https://godboxtours.com for further information.

Airport

Ghana has two airports: Kotoka International Airport (ACC) located in Accra (Ghana's capitol), and the Kumasi Airport (KMS), located in Kumasi, which is the capitol of the Ashanti Region. The Kumasi airport currently has ongoing construction to develop the Kumasi Airport into Kumasi International Airport, scheduled to fully conclude by the end of 2021.

When packing for your travels, do yourself a big favor and do not bring a lot of suitcases or overstuff your suitcases. If you do, you will get "broke off" in heavy baggage fees. You don't want to be that person that has to step to the side and try to shift weight between suitcases and or your carryon bag. Or be heartbroken because your carryon is not in compliance and the airline makes you check the bag at additional cost.

So before you go getting all excited and buying up new suitcases, check the rules and regulations of the airline on which you will be flying. Some airlines do allow concessions for checked boxes if you have a few things that you really want to bring over via the airplane. If you are thinking about doing this call your airline to see if they offer this service and obtain their rules and regulations (i.e., box size, weight, etc.).

If you have NEVER flown before please, please go online and read the policies and restrictions for things you can and cannot take onboard or check in. There are rules for what size liquids you can place in your carry on or purse as well as the size of your carryon bag. This may seem like a "no brainer" to those of us who fly often, but for someone who has not flown in many years or not at all, the airport will be a real learning curve.

Taxes

Moving to Ghana does not mean that you no longer have to pay your home country's taxes. You are still a citizen of your home country and must adhere by its tax rules. If you have an online business or are able to telework for one of your home country's companies while in Ghana, make sure you pay your home country taxes.

Now for a real sucker punch to your gut; while in Ghana or other countries, if you earn income, certain home countries require you to report that income and pay taxes on those earnings (to include business owners). This may be good or bad news for you. For instance, if you are a U.S. citizen, and you are below the threshold of required earnings (most fall here), you may be excluded from paying. However, if you are really rolling in the dinero, you "gonna" pay the cost to be the boss.

Resource:

> U.S. citizens may reference this link: https://www.irs.gov/individuals/international-taxpayers/foreign-earned-income-exclusion

All others do your due diligence and check with your home country's tax agency for pertinent information.

Berakah Infinity Foundation

Don't forget to inform and Share the nonprofit Berakah Infinity Foundation Link with Friends and Family. Visit https://berakahinfinity.org to learn more.

So you want to move to Ghana? Then come on over.

Ghana says, Akwaaba (welcome)! She is far from perfect and has lots of work yet to be done, but man, I'm loving Ghana!

What are you standing around idle for? Hopefully you already have your passport and it will not expire within the next 6 months. Hurry up, get those passport photos taken (don't forget to pack extras for future documents) and apply for your visa.

After all, Ghana is waiting!

Resources

I Got My Freedom LTD
igmf@freedomland.com

TYPE DATE HERE   *Insert Company Logo*

The Comptroller General
Ghana Immigration Service
Accra, Ghana

Dear Sir,

APPLICATION FOR WORK AND RESIDENCE PERMIT

TYPE YOUR WHOLE NAME HERE   AMERICAN

TYPE 2nd OWNER WHOLE NAME HERE IF APPLICABLE   UNITED KINGDOM

We wish to apply for work and residence permit for the above named American and U.K. nationals who are directors and shareholders of our company.

Our company was legally incorporated under the Companies Act of Ghana on *DATE COMPANY WAS REGISTERED IN GHANA* to undertake the below:

a. Agriculture
b. Cleaning services

To enable *NAMES LISTED ABOVE* to start work legally in Ghana, we hereby request your office to grant appropriate authorization to them. This permit will pave way for us to complete other statutory compliance requirement imposed on our company.

Please find attached the necessary supporting documents for your perusal.

Thank you.

Sincerely,

_____
YOUR NAME HERE *(sign above)*
Founder/Director, I Got My Freedom LTD

Resources | 129

References

NIA, Foreigners Identification Management System F.M.S., fims.org.gh/info/where-to-buy-a-card/. Accessed 26 April 2021.

"How to Obtain a Work and Residence Permit." *FIRMUS Advisory,* firmusadvisory.com/2021/05/28/how-to-obtain-a-work-and-residence-permit-in-ghana/. Accessed 28 April 2021.

Taxpayer Identification Number. *Ghana Revenue Authority*, gra.gov.gh/tin/. Accessed 28 April 2021.

"Top 10 Waste Management Challenges Ghana Must Overcome." *Energy Digital Magazine,* 7 July 2014, energydigital.com/top-10/top-10-waste-management-challenges-ghana-must-overcome. Accessed 21 May 2021.

Ghana Lands Commission. www.lc.gov.gh/. Accessed 23 February 2021.

Accra Metropolitan Assembly, www.ama.gov.gh/building-permit.php. Accessed March 2021.

Driver and Vehicle Licensing Authority (DVLA), dvla.gov.gh/services.php. Accessed June 2021.

Yeung, Peter. "The Toxic Effects of Electronic Waste in Accra, Ghana." *Bloomberg CityLab*, 29 May 2019, www.bloomberg.com/news/articles/2019-05-29/the-rich-world-s-electronic-wastedumped-in-ghana. Extracted 18 March 2021.

Donkor, Jonathan. "Clean-up at Agbobloshie Market Progresses." *Ghanaian Times,* 9 July 2021.

Sri, Mathias. "Ghana's Way Towards Sustainable e-waste Recycling-First Country in Africa to Officially Launch Guidelines for Environmentally Sound e-waste Management." *e-waste Sustainable Recycling Industries (SRI)*, 5 March 2018, www.sustainable-recycling.org/ghanas-way-towards-sustainable-e-waste-recycling-first-country-in-africa-to-officially-launch-guidelines-for-environmentally-sound-e-waste-management/. Accessed 4 May 2021.

"Customs Agents." Ghana Revenue Authority. gra.gov.gh/customs/customs-agents/

"Dual Nationality/Citizenship." Ministry of the Interior Republic of Ghana, www.mint.gov.gh/services/dual-nationality-citizenship/. Accessed 2 March 2021.

Pheko, Motsoko, "Effects of Colonialism on Africa's Past and Present." Pambazuka News. 31 May 2012, www.pambazuka.org/node/80292. Extracted 27 June 2021.

The Parliament of the Republic of Ghana. "Renewable Energy Act 2011 (Act 832)." Ghana Publishing Company LTD: 31 December 2011, Assembly Press, Accra, Ghana.

"Ghana Striving for an Industrialized Economy Driven by Nuclear, Renewable Energy." GhanaWeb. 27 June 2021, www.ghanaweb.com/GhanaHomePage/business/Ghana-striving-for-an-industrialised-economy-driven-by-nuclear-renewable-energy-1296031.

Misachi, John. "Countries with Most Nuclear Power Plants." World Atlas. 13 September 2018, www.worldatlas.com/articles/countries-with-the-most-nuclear-power-plants.html. Extracted 1 July

Country Profile Ghana. *International Hydropower Association*. May 2019, www.hydropower.org/country-profiles/ghana.

About the Author

Hannah P. Yacob is an ardent Torah keeper, former educator and Education Counselor. She is also an author and valuable advocate of the Berakah Infinity Foundation.

The author currently resides in Ghana with her husband.

Acknowledgments

A big thank you goes out to my late parents and grandparents who were always, and even in death continue to be an inspiration to me. Special thanks to my patient husband who allowed me to pick his brain relentlessly for the valuable expertise brought forth in Chapter 7. He, who did not complain when I requested further insight and explanation in order to relay the information more clearly to all of us mere mortal, non-engineers. Your encouragement is endless, and is much appreciated.

CPSIA information can be obtained
at www.ICGtesting.com
Printed in the USA
LVHW080041191021
700772LV00013B/565